BEYOND
TECHNIQUE

Also by Lawrence LeShan:

An Ethic for the Age of Space

The Psychology of War

The Dilemma of Psychology

Cancer as a Turning Point

The Science of the Paranormal

The Mechanic and the Gardener

Einstein's Space and Van Gogh's Sky
(with Henry Margenau)

You Can Fight for Your Life

Alternate Realities

How to Meditate

The Medium, the Mystic, and the Physicist

Psychosomatic Aspects of Neoplastic Disease
(with David Kissen)

Counseling the Dying
(with Edgar Jackson, Margarita Bowers, and
James Knight)

BEYOND TECHNIQUE

Psychotherapy for the 21st Century

Lawrence LeShan, Ph.D.

JASON ARONSON INC.
Northvale, New Jersey
London

The author gratefully acknowledges permission to reprint lines from *Report to Greco*, by Nikos Kazantzakis, translated from the Greek by P. A. Bien. Copyright © 1961, copyright renewed 1993 by Helen N. Kazantzakis. English translation, Copyright © 1965 by Simon & Schuster. Reprinted with permission of the publisher.

Production Editor: Elaine Lindenblatt

This book was set in 11 pt. New Aster by Alpha Graphics of Pittsfield, New Hampshire, and printed and bound by Book-mart Press of North Bergen, New Jersey.

Copyright © 1996 by Lawrence LeShan

10 9 8 7 6 5 4 3 2 1

Library of Congress Cataloging-in-Publication Data

LeShan, Lawrence L., 1920–
    Beyond technique : psychotherapy for the 21st century /
by Lawrence LeShan.
        p. cm.
    Includes bibliographical references and index.
    ISBN 1-56821-550-9 (alk. paper)
    1. Psychotherapy—Philosophy. I. Title.
RC437.5.L47   1996
616.89'14'01—dc20   95-10750

Manufactured in the United States of America. Jason Aronson Inc. offers books and cassettes. For information and catalog write to Jason Aronson Inc., 230 Livingston Street, Northvale, New Jersey 07647.

To
Anne Appelbaum
who taught me about the infinite variety
of human encounters
and the hope and courage needed
to strive to become truly individual

CONTENTS

ACKNOWLEDGMENTS

I have been very lucky in the teachers I have had. These have included Dick Henneman, Arthur Jenness, Abraham Meyerson, Abe Maslow, Alfred Korzybski, Marthe Gassmann, Anne Appelbaum and many others. The patients who have taught me are too many to mention and their names are not for me to use here. Eda LeShan has been a major contributor to my understanding and a major support of my work. I owe a large debt to the Fordham Library at Lincoln Center and the Centerville Public Library in Cape Cod. Without their open and positive attitude toward students like myself, this book could not have been written.

For a long time—for half a century in fact—psychiatry tried to interpret the human mind merely as a mechanism and consequently the therapy of mental disease merely in terms of technique. I believe that this dream has been dreamt out. What now begins to loom on the horizon are not the sketches of a psychologized medicine, but rather those of a humanized psychiatry.

A doctor, however, who would still interpret his own role mainly as that of a technician would confess that he sees in his patient nothing more than a machine, instead of seeing the human being behind the disease.

Our generation is realistic for we have come to know man as he really is. After all, man is that being who invented the gas chambers of Auschwitz; however, he is also that being who entered these gas chambers upright, with the Lord's Prayer or the *Shema Yisrael* on his lips.

Victor Frankl

1

THE VIEW FROM 1995

Since the beginning of this century, we have been experimenting with and developing a special approach to try to improve the human condition. We call this psychotherapy. Now, after all this work, it is time for a fresh look at where we came from, what we are trying to do, to what degree our methods and goals are in accord with each other, and how successful we are in reaching our goals.

Since 1900 the number of recognized professionals in the field has increased tremendously. From a few psychiatrists, working mostly in asylums, at the beginning of the century we have come to the hundreds of thousands of social workers, psychologists, and psychiatrists in private practice today in addition to the many working in universities, clinics, and mental hospitals. Further, there are ministers, nurse practitioners, and other professionals using the techniques that we have developed. In the rush and activity of this development, we have not stopped very often to ask ourselves the basic questions about our assumptions, goals, and techniques and to what degree we were clear about our course. Abraham Maslow, who tried hard to provide some clarity on these matters, once compared us to an airline pilot who radioed back to his home base, "We're lost but we're making wonderful time."

There is also so much about the process of psychotherapy that we have learned in the past hundred years and that we rarely, if ever, put into practice. We know how to do our work far better than we actually do it.

The purpose of this book is to look very briefly at where we came from and the assumptions from these sources that are still part of our thinking and thereby affect our work. I will then show that our methods do not always lead to our goals and describe the redefinition of psychotherapy necessary to bring our field successfully into the new era that is now arriving.

Our profession as psychotherapists is a very old and honorable one. One half of our ancestry is from medicine. In the other we are descended from the wise men and women of the tribes and villages and later from the spiritual directors of organized religion. We are very much in line with the Western spiritual tradition. "Each one," wrote Spinoza, "should learn to love his own utility." In St. Thomas Aquinas's terms, each one of us should try to fulfill his or her own nature. The heart of the Western tradition is that we each, at birth, are given a seed as a gift—our soul. Our task is to grow and garden the seed so that when the gift is called back, it will be worthy of The One who has given and recalled it. It is this type of goal—that all should love their own utility, achieve their own nature, grow to the fullest of their potential—that we try, as psychotherapists to help people achieve. In order to remind himself and his patients of the spiritual nature of our kind of work, Carl Jung had a sign over the entrance to his consulting room. The sign said in Latin that whether or not He was called, God would be present in the session. *Vocatus atque Non-Vocatus, Deus aderit.*

This basic aspect of Western spirituality ties our work as therapists very closely into the heart of Western religious thought. In his novel about St. Francis of Assisi, Nikos Kazantzakis (1957) put a haiku into the saint's mouth.

> I said to the almond tree,
> "Sister, speak to me of God."
> And the almond tree blossomed.

And in our work when we are providing an environment and relationship within which the patient can blossom, can fulfill his or her being, we are, from a Western viewpoint, talking about God.

We work hard at our craft and deeply care about it. Our results are far lower than we would wish.

Our models and methods vary widely. Some of us talk a lot during a session; some of us are mostly silent. Some of us deal primarily with the past, some primarily with the present. Some of us say, "Uh huh" in seven different ways; some of us say things like "Ach zo, it is your oedipal conflict." Some of us may put an arm around the shoulder of a patient as we walk him to the door after a painful session. Some of us would never do this. Some see patients one at a time; some work with the entire family or with a group. (My first teacher of psychotherapy started the course by saying, "There are two ways of doing therapy. Indiwidually or groupily!" Today we know that there are many variations on both.)

Not only our methods but also the basic models we use vary widely. Freud used the mechanical model of his time (as did Marx and Darwin). Some of us use a biological model, some a switchboard (or now a computer) model, the emergence model of Humanistic Psychology, or any one of a number of others.

All methods and models seem to get about the same results.

When there are results, there is one thing that all methods and models have in common. We have been modeling.

We *listen* to the patient and thus, by example, teach him to listen to himself. We *care* for the patient and thus teach him to care for himself. We *have hopes* for the patient and thereby teach him to have hopes for himself. We *respect* the patient and thereby teach him to respect himself.

Is this the common factor? But we do these much more often than we get results. Our results are sporadic and apparently unpredictable. But we do these things regularly. *Or do we?*

Let us look deeper. We come from a synthesis of wisdom-seeking in the great tradition and of medical science. Freud laid the foundations of all modern psychotherapy, and he was a trained physician. Many of the assumptions of medical science underlie our work today.

In medical science we do something or provide something to cure the patient of his ills. We may make wry jokes about this like repeating Voltaire's comment that the task of the physician is to amuse the patient while nature heals him, but this concept of doing something or providing something to cure the patient is central to most of our professional actions.

But *what* do we provide? There is an old idea in medicine that somewhere there exists one substance or herb or procedure, an elixir, that will cure all our ills. This idea goes back at least to Sumerian times—we find it in the Gilgamish epic. This is an idea that medicine has long since given up. We now are clear that different substances and procedures are needed for different medical conditions. The search for a universal elixir has long been abandoned in medicine. My physician will treat me very differently each time I come in with a different problem. At various visits to the office, I may get a medical prescription (and these come in a tremendous variety of forms), a splint for a broken bone, a surgical procedure, a new diet, a referral to a specialist (with her variety of actions), a recommendation to rest or to exercise more, and so on and so on.

But what about psychotherapy? In school we were taught about many methods, their assumptions and techniques, their values and liabilities.

Then, think back to when you started actually working with patients. Your mentor, your supervisor, generally made it plain that there is a right way to do therapy. Learn it, you were told implicitly and explicitly, and do it well enough and you would cure all those who were curable.

But isn't there a correct model and a resulting correct method? After all, our teachers taught us that this was so. (All schools do this. Questions concerning the basic assumptions and model used by a psychotherapy school are questioned in that school about as often as the Ossavatore Romano questions the historical existence of Jesus.)

However, let us step back again. Think about yourself for a moment. What type of therapy, relationship with the therapist, frequency of sessions, length of sessions would be ideal to help *you* flourish, grow best, become most fully?

Now think of someone you know very well. A spouse or "important other" or someone like that. Would they flourish and grow best with the same psychotherapy design and metaphor that you yourself would? And, if not, why should all your patients need the same design if you and your spouse do not?

Let us conceive of an ideal psychotherapy practice. A special and wonderful group of people have come to you for therapy. On Monday morning you have Anna Karenina; on Monday afternoon, Scarlett O'Hara; on Tuesday, Iago; on Wednesday, Madame Emma Bovary; on Wednesday afternoon, Raskolnikov; on Thursday, Hamlet; and on Friday, George F. Babbitt. Do you really believe that the same, identical model of what a human being is and how a psychotherapy session should be conducted would be best for all these seven? Stop a moment and think about this as a professional. For each of these individuals to flourish most fully through the therapy, would they need the *same* behavior of the therapist, frequency and length of sessions, and theoretical and metaphor model?

Each of your patients, however, is as unique, complex, and deep in their abilities to feel, hurt, have joys, hopes, and fears as any of these literary fictional characters. The difference is that in fiction they are delineated more clearly and sharply, and you know them in their contrasts and shadings. If you would, ideally at least, treat *them* differently, do you carry these differences to the real patients who come to see you?

The man who taught Abe Maslow many of the basic concepts of Humanistic Psychology was the psychiatrist Kurt Goldstein. (Among other things, he coined the term *self-actualization*.) When a patient was coming to see him, Goldstein would first take a moment alone and say to himself, "Now I must rid myself of all my pre-conceptions."

Most of us, however, do nothing like this. We do not prepare ourselves to be surprised by a new patient. And when we do not do as Goldstein did, we say that we are assuming that the patient will adjust himself to our favorite metaphor, model and method. That these are so dependable and universally valid that we know in advance that using them is better for the patient than would be our asking ourselves, "What does *this* patient need?" Medicine may have given up the search for a universal elixir, but have we?

As one example of these preconceptions, where did we *ever* get the idea that one hour or fifty minutes is the best time allotment for all or at least most of our patients?

This is a difficult point for we psychotherapists and counselors. Let us look at it once more. How many of us when a patient leaves the office after the first visit ask ourself, "What type of therapeutic technique, model, or metaphor does *this* patient need to flourish most fully?" Sir William Osler said, in a famous statement, "It is more important to know what sort of patient has the disease than what sort of disease the patient has." If he was right, what are the implications for our work?

Many years ago I was present at a famous, very psy-choanalytically oriented child guidance clinic. There was an invited speaker, Dr. Anina Brandt, a child psy-chiatrist. She was speaking of what the world is like to a child, the long, long thoughts, the sudden changes in mood that seem to change the color of the entire world, the strange behavior of the grown-ups who claimed to be consistent but seemed to behave otherwise, and so forth. It was, for me, a very moving talk, but the staff were becoming more and more uncomfortable. Finally one of them interrupted and asked, "Dr. Brandt, what *school* do you belong to?" Brandt became confused and answered, "But how can I know until I see the child?"

Don't we all really know, even if we do not act very much on the knowledge, that there are psychoanalytic patients, Jungian patients, Adlerian, Existentialist patients, and, the most prevalent, the GOK ("God Only Knows") patients.

The great teachers of Western mysticism were very aware of this. Rabbi Nachman said, "God calls one man with a shout, one with a song, one with a whisper." St. Theresa of Liseaux wrote that the hardest task of the spiritual advisor, "harder than making the sun rise at night, is to give up one's own special likes and dislikes and to lead this person along the special path that Christ has appointed to lead him to God." The founder of Hassidic mysticism, the Baal Shem Tov, said, "Since the dawn of creation no two people have been born alike. Each is unique. It is the task of each to further this uniqueness. And it is the failure to work on this task which has held back the coming of the Messiah." Thomas Merton (1961) quotes, with much approval, the Benedictine mystic Dom Augustine Baker:

> The director is not to teach his own way, nor indeed any determinate way of prayer, but instruct his disciples how they may themselves find out the way proper for them. . . . In a word, he is only God's usher and must lead souls on God's way, not his own. [p. 20]

In Merton's view, spiritual direction consists in helping each person develop in his own way, to that "supreme work of art" that is theirs and theirs alone. It is the work "of rescuing the inner man from automatism" (p. 22). The spiritual director is concerned with "the *whole person*" and not just with spiritual aspects alone. Merton points out that you do not go to a spiritual director to take care of your spirit as you would to a dentist to take care of your teeth or a barber to get a haircut but to help you on the proper road for you as an individual to develop in your way.

For therapists, I strongly recommend the following exercises. (They will be much more effective if you do them with paper and pencil rather than in your head.)

I. A. Think about yourself for a moment. After writing your name, write a two- or three-sentence description of yourself as objectively as you can. Then very briefly describe the therapeutic situation in which you, as a patient, would be most likely to thrive; to blossom and grow in *your* individual direction, what kind of therapist and what kind of relationship with him or her would be best for you?

  B. Now select a member of your family and repeat the procedure completely.

  C. Now select a patient with whom you have been working for a significant time. Repeat the procedure exactly. Then write how this ideal differs from the real therapeutic situation he or she is in.

  D. What, if any, are your conclusions from the above? Are any changes called for? If so, do you think you will make them? If not (honestly, now), why not?

Recently I was doing a workshop with a few hundred full-time therapists. After doing this exercise, I told them about the ideal practice I wrote of earlier.

I asked them to select two of the fictional patients on the list and describe on paper the ideal therapeutic situation, the best ecological niche for each of the two—

to describe the best-for-them relationship, pacing, and so forth. Then we discussed the question "If these two patients came to you, would you provide this environment, or are you so ingrained in the method you have been taught that you would use it on them also?" The overwhelming response was the sad statement that they knew each of the patients needed (for best thriving) a special therapeutic environment, but they would not provide it and would use their accustomed methods, relationship, and pacing with them. We all found this a depressing and discouraging picture.

In terms of our history as psychotherapists being one half from medicine, it may be interesting to compare some aspects of a typical medical practice and a typical psychotherapy practice.

Physician	Psychotherapist
1. Frequently refers patients to specialists in other areas	1. Rarely refers patients
2. Different amounts of time assigned to patients with different conditions	2. Patients generally given the same amount of time
3. Different procedures with patients with different problems	3. Typically uses same procedure with all or most patients
4. Clear as to goal—curing	4. Often unclear if goal is curing or healing

Ian Gawlor has put the problem in his usual succinct way. "The question is," he said, "are you committed to a method or to a patient?" (personal communication, 1994). Most of us have believed we were committed to our patients, but our behavior, alas, has indicated otherwise.

Another useful exercise for psychotherapists was taught to me forty years ago by my first control therapist, Marthe Gassmann.

II. On a sheet of lined paper, draw two vertical lines from the top to the bottom. Leave about an inch from the left-hand margin for the first. Then divide the remaining space in half with the other line. In the first, narrow column, write the names of six of your regular patients, several lines apart.

Now in the first broad column, opposite each name, write how the patient changed or what he or she learned through the work in the past months.

After you have completed this for all the patients listed, go to the second broad column. In this write how *you* changed through this particular relationship, what *you* have learned from it.

A therapeutic relationship is a dynamic Gestalt. One part of it cannot undergo meaningful changes without the other parts being affected. If there is material only in the "how the patient changed" column and none in the "how you changed" one, it is quite likely that the patient's growth and changes are built on sand and will collapse in the near future.

If there are *no* changes in the last six months, I would like to suggest you read Freud's paper called "Analysis Terminable and Interminable." In it he suggests that if the patient shows no progress in six months, the *analyst* should go back into therapy. If there is no change in this period, I strongly urge that, at the very least, you examine the situation in detail with your supervisor. And if you do not have a supervisor, you are far, far overdue to get one.

An interesting and often useful exercise for a therapist who is troubled about a particular patient is to ask
the following questions. (As with most exercises of this
general type, it will be far more effective if done with
pen and paper rather than just within your own head.)

1. How is this person most like all other persons?
2. How is he most like other members of his subculture?
3. How is he most like himself—what are his individual
   characteristics?
4. Suppose he were farther along his path in the development of his uniqueness and individuality. How
   would he be?
5. What does he need to do in order to move in this
   direction?
6. What type of therapeutic environment would be
   most conducive to his growth in this way?

We come here to an old philosophical problem that
William James fought against the philosophers Lotze,
Royce, and Bradley. This is the false dichotomy between, as James put it, "utter unity and utter irrele-
vance." Our patients *are* all different, but they share
many things. They are most like all other humans in
some aspects, most like some others in some aspects,
most like themselves in some aspects. They all belong
to the same species and were raised under the same sky.
They all need both relationship and solitude (but a different percentage of each for each individual); they are
shaped by their individual genetics, early experience,
culture, subculture, family, and so forth. Each is an
individual; each resembles and reacts like and unlike
the other. They resemble each other as do two superb
poems or two superb symphonies. The healthier they

are, the more they are distinct and yet retain their commonalities. The task of the therapist is to help in this individuation. Our patients should be far more unique and distinguishable from each other *after* the therapy than they were before it.

There is an old symbol, used by both the Pythagoreans in Hellenistic Greece and the early Christians. It is the *Y*. The place where the three lines meet stands for the present moment in time. At any moment, including this one, you have three choices. You can return (go back down the base leg of the *Y*) and stay as you are and have been. Let your accustomed masks and roles continue to dominate your life. Or, you can permit the present situation to determine your actions and reactions and let your personality be shaped by the demands and expectations of others and by what is going on in your body and around you. That is choosing the left-hand arm of the *Y*. Or, you can determine that you will grow and become in *your* way, that you will control your actions and personality. That is going on the right-hand arm. Every moment, says this viewpoint, is a *kairos* moment: a moment of portentious choice for the future. Reports of survivors of the *Gulags* showed that some emerged from this crisis unchanged, almost as if it were a gratuitous experience. Some were weakened or destroyed by it. Some grew and became much more from the experience. I have seen the same thing in cancer survivors. The task of the therapist, it seems to me, is to be aware of the possibilities and help the patient to the right arm of the *Y*.

———•———

Let us look deeper into the medical model that has influenced us so strongly and many of whose assumptions are still part of our everyday work. That these assumptions are often unverbalized makes their influence even more powerful.

The goal in the medical model is to cure: to relieve symptoms or system failure. Health is seen as present when there are no painful or disturbing symptoms or indications of danger of system failure. Health is defined as the absence of sickness.

In psychotherapy this has essentially been translated to mean that health is present when there is no special psychic pain and there is effectiveness of functioning in society. Freud expressed this (on what we may assume was a gray and gloomy day in Vienna) when he said that the goal of psychoanalysis is "to remove the special pain of the patient and return him to that unhappiness common to mankind"! Freud had, as we see, his bad days even as you and I.

One problem with this definition of health—the absence of special psychic pain and effectiveness of functioning in society—is that it defines as healthy the successful manipulative psychopath and the chameleon of the other-directed personality. On the other hand, the struggling artist, groping and suffering to express a dimly perceived vision, trying to help the world's inhabitants see themselves and the rest of reality more deeply, is defined as sick. He or she often suffers much psychic pain and may not be very effective in functioning in society. A Van Gogh or a Mozart is seen as more sick than a junk-bond Milliken or than the rich and successful corrupt ex-presidents of many failed savings and loan companies for whose failure the rest of us are paying in our taxes.

We as psychotherapists do not really believe this definition of cure, but it does influence us and makes many of our problems worse. It confuses us as to what we are really trying to do in our work and therefore the methods we use to accomplish this.

The medical approach is based on curing. Few of us would care to define ourselves as curers and not healers.

We all know what it means to cure. It means to apply a procedure or a substance that will stop symptoms or system failure, that will, in our terms, "ease psychic pain and/or increase social effectiveness"; the ability to survive and prosper in society.

That is what it means to cure. But what does it mean to heal? In our work it means to help the patient grow toward greater zest, enthusiasm, joy in life. To become more and more fully him- or herself and unique. Karen Horney expressed this in her definition of psychotherapy: "the attempt to help the patient take his neurosis, his uniqueness, his individuality, from the front of the face where it acts as blinders and move it around to the back of the neck where it can act as an outboard motor." Freud's definition was that of curing. Horney's was that of healing.

In the high days of psychoanalysis earlier in the century, its practitioners regarded it as divine revelation. (Will Durant in those days defined psychoanalysis by saying, "It is not an art and it is not a science. It is the defense of a hero.") At that time, one of the great minds in the mental health field was Trigant Burrow. Psychotherapy, he wrote (1932), must avoid the errors of most educational systems—that its goal is to develop individuals who will fit into the local cultural system with as little pain as possible and function "normally" in the system. "This implies," he said, "that the society is healthy and fitting into it is right for all persons" (p. 24). (I might point out here that this viewpoint is very close to that of the diagnosis of "sluggish schizophrenia" used in Stalinist Russia. The primary symptom of this diagnosis was either a belief that you could improve the system or a belief that the decisions of the Central Committee were open to question.)

Burrow said that this view did violence to the uniqueness of each person and his unique path to zest and enthusiasm. "Normality is a shared illness," he wrote (p. 24).

In this context, it may be helpful to consider the idea that anyone who wants to make things better than they are is, by definition, a rebel. And that a rebel who is not in trouble with the local system is laying down on the job!

Burrow, admiring Freud above all other men, said that he was like Newton, whose approach and system was first thought to apply to all of reality. After Planck and Einstein, we saw that Newton's view was valid but limited to one segment of reality only and that other models were needed for the rest. So, said Burrow, Freud's concepts were first believed to apply to all of our psychological life. Later work showed it to be valid for only one part and that other models were needed for the rest. Freud's model was not the sun in the center of the psychological solar system but only a major planet. The correspondence of the times showed that this idea did not please Freud at all.

In healing, our goal is not even to make the person less crazy, but to make him more successfully crazy in his own special way and style.

William Alanson White has somewhere remarked that most of us are pretty normal in most areas. Then there are a few areas in which we are either neurotic or eccentric depending on our financial standing. In each of us, further, is one area in which we are frankly psychotic. The task of us adults, said White, is to recognize this area and either compensate our behavior for it so that we do not get into trouble or, preferably, learn how to use our particular craziness in our own service—in the pursuit of our life goals.

We cannot *heal* a person by applying a general usage procedure or substance. We cannot manipulate someone into healing. There is no metaphor or method that will serve as a universal elixir for healing. We cannot heal the patient by doing something to him or her.

This is why there is a basic rule in psychotherapy—Miale's Law, named after the psychotherapist Florence Miale who first put it in these words: "Any response of the therapist which comes from technique rather than from human feeling is antitherapeutic" (personal communication, 1965).

But we can provide an environment, a specially designed *climate* in which this particular patient can flourish and heal. In this environment we, and our relationship with the patient, are a major part.

We can fix a Chevrolet and cure its problems. To do this we apply standard procedures and substances (e.g., change a spark plug and put in oil). To heal a person, we must garden him, provide a special place and environment designed for his needs so that he can grow past his pain and blockages—an environment in which he can, in Horney's words, make his individuality into an outboard motor.

A gardener plants arbor vitae deep in the ground, plants juniper shallowly with part sun and part shade, plants mountain laurel in the shade and pachysandra near pine trees. She wishes her plants to flourish, each in its own way, so she treats them differently in a manner inclined to let them do this. We wish for our patients what the gardener wishes for her plants. Do we treat them as she does?

Practically speaking, what does all of this mean?

Patient 1: Maureen

Maureen's mother was a classic paranoid personality. From the beginning she constantly found fault with Maureen and accused her of all sorts of negative motivations for anything she did or did not do. Her father was very passive. Three younger children all developed into inadequate characters when they grew up and never were able to establish long-term relationships or remain at the same jobs for very long. Her mother started her in ice skating classes at age 3 and announced that Maureen would become an Olympic champion. A battle was joined over food with the mother constantly saying she was too fat and Maureen stealing food. At 7 the mother put her on drugs (Dexedrine) to help her lose weight, and Maureen was shortly addicted. By 16 she was suffering from hallucinations and was hospitalized and given shock treatment. Quite incidentally, while she was in the hospital she received no Dexedrine and, after suffering severe withdrawal symptoms, recovered and had no further hallucinations.

She became a CPA and, in the office alone with the door closed, felt safe. Only there did she feel secure. She never had any close relationships and believed that anyone who came close to her would naturally try to improve her. Very deeply she felt unacceptable and that something was very wrong with her. Any attempt at improving her was, to her, a clear statement that this fantasy was valid and that the other person agreed with it.

She had had, over the course of the years, a good deal of psychotherapy ranging from a four-year, full scale, old-style analysis (four times a week, on the couch, etc.) to a two-year course of art therapy. She felt that she had received no benefit from any of this work. She had frequent depressions in which she would just stay in bed for several weeks. Every time she visited her mother and the two sisters who were still living at home in Montana (three or four times a year), she would return extremely depressed. On returning to her New York apartment, she felt wounded, guilty, and full of self-hate. She lived largely on junk food and was fifty to seventy-five pounds overweight at all times.

What she apparently needed was a soft, gently non-explorative, noninterpretative milieu. Any interpretation was seen as another attempt to change and improve her as her mother had done since she was a child. She needed an environment that was loving and that respected her for her struggle to survive. This was easy to do as she had fought very hard and successfully against great odds to survive. There could be no psychotherapeutic pressure of any kind. The pace of psychotherapy—how often and how long sessions were—had to be limited with this addictive woman as it could have replaced food as the comforter. We had learned (by the 1930s, at any rate) not to let life revolve around therapy instead of vice versa.

At one session she told me that she felt that she had made no progress in her work with me. Instead of looking at the anger in this (as I might have done with many other patients) or looking back to earlier times in her life when she had felt the same way (as I might have done with others), I listened, told her, and made her see that I knew how she felt, pointed out some progress (as in the shorter periods of depression), and repeated how strong and brave she had been to have come so far. She relaxed, and the subject was not brought up again.

After a half year or so of this approach, she began to blossom. She was no longer wounded by her visits to Montana but came back filled with pity and compassion for her Eugene O'Neill type of family instead of guilt and self-hatred. For the first time when she feels depressed, she gets out of bed in a day or two instead of after several weeks. When she feels low, she now looks to buying new music tapes, taking new university courses, and buying new clothes instead of to eating. She has lost about thirty-five pounds. After living for over ten years in an apartment with the rather decrepit furniture that was there when she moved in, she has furnished and fixed up the place and now "loves it." She says her life is richer than it has ever been before. She still has a long way to go, as do we all.

Patient 2: Ralph

Working in the outpatient clinic of a court-of-last-resort cancer center, I kept hearing rumors about a new patient, a lawyer with a vicious sarcastic tongue who kept asking everyone there all sorts of questions about their work and about the clinic in general. The laboratory staff had threatened to resign as a group unless the director forbade him to go in there again. I knew only this of him and that he had an extremely malignant tumor that as with most of our patients, mainline medicine had very little left to offer.

One day, doing some paperwork in my office, with the door slightly open, he came in, shut the door behind him, sat down in the chair across from mine, and said, "I want you to help me lick this cancer in my gut. Can we start now or do I have to be formal and make an appointment?"

I answered (having been in the field long enough to have learned the danger of making implied promises I might not be able to keep), "I'll help you fight it. I can't promise to help you lick it."

He answered, "I'll lick it. I have always been able to do anything I wanted to."

Feeling it important to stay on the level he was setting (and possibly a little angry at this approach), I said, "Then I guess you weren't very good at deciding what you wanted to do since your life led you to my office."

We went on from there and got along famously!

I have never in my life met a more aggressive man. He was angry down to his toes as near as I could tell. He had always loved music, but his parents had insisted that this was no career for a man and that he must follow his father's footsteps and become a lawyer. He did. In his law school there had been a custom for over forty years of the senior class writing a musical cabaret about their law school experience. In his senior year, he wrote the libretto, words, and music and directed it. It was so vicious, so hurtfully hostile to the staff and the school, that the custom was abandoned and never done again.

He was extremely successful as a lawyer. His superbly high intelligence, along with an energy level far above that of most people and his aggressive approach to anything he did, made him a very valued member of his firm in spite of the fact that practically everyone there disliked him.

He was married to a woman from the country club set of eastern Long Island. They had a house with a swimming pool, two children, a Lincoln, and a Buick station wagon. He and his wife had both gotten what they wanted: he a rich wife with entry into the best country clubs and she a rising and successful lawyer. The major emotion they felt for each other was somewhere between dislike and hatred.

Softness and gentleness made him frightened and therefore even more angry. He was afraid that he would destroy anyone close to him unless they were at least as tough as he was. His anger had to be met strongly, not passively accepted. He needed an environment in which he could explore ways of relating to others without fear of destroying them or arousing even more rejection than he already felt that the world had given him. He needed to be met strongly and with respect for his ability to take it as well as to dish it out. He let me know in no uncertain terms when I missed something or was wrong in an interpretation. I returned the compliment in the same terms. He did not need a therapist who was an uncle or a father or mother figure but rather one who was a comrade-in-arms, working by his side for *his* goals. Being part of the environment this man needed was something like being in a small boat at sea during a hurricane!

After three years of this, he has changed his life completely. He is divorced (to the expressed great relief of both his wife and his children) and lives alone in a furnished apartment. He works two days a week as a legal consultant for a manufacturing firm. The rest of the time he spends in writing music, which is of a high enough caliber that several of his works have been played by major European and American symphony orchestras, and in conducting a small but very good orchestra. He reads very widely in the classics and has written two (unpublished) novels and published several short stories. He regards his life as rich and fulfilling.

Patient 3: Martin

Martin was in his late thirties when I first saw him. He was divorced and had one daughter who lived with her mother and saw him on occasional weekends. He was an associate professor of business management in a middle-sized college in a large East Coast city. He had been teaching the same courses for nearly fifteen years. There was nothing particularly wrong with him—no especial symptoms of psychic pain, social dysfunction, or physical problems, but, as he put it later, "There was nothing particularly right with me or my life, either." He spent his vacations at singles hotels in the mountains that he described as "pleasantly promiscuous."

He had several women friends and generally mild, rather friendly, long-term affairs with two of them. He would have four to six shorter affairs each year. These varied from one-night stands to several months in length. He had no close men friends. He was witty and intelligent and was frequently invited to dinner parties by relatives or acquaintances who either needed an extra man for the evening or had a woman friend or relative they wanted him to meet. He enjoyed these social events but "made sure that they came to nothing." He had once been to a swingers club that featured a nightly orgy, enjoyed it, but never returned. When questioned about this, he would tell the story of Voltaire who went to an orgy, aquitted himself magnificently, and refused to go again with the statement "Once, a philosopher. Twice, a pervert."

When the fad was at its height, he took up jogging. Later, in keeping with many in his social class, he switched to tennis. He read very little, mostly popular novels and newspapers. He watched a good deal of television.

In short, in the words that Tolstoy used to describe the life of Ivan Ilych, "his life was most ordinary and there-fore most terrible." It was pleasant, highly socially accept-able, busy, and essentially meaningless. He had found a way of life that made no demands on him and that was unrelated to his own particular, unique being.

The summer he was thirty-seven he decided to take part of his vacation on a walking tour of New England instead of in his usual manner. (He recently had seen the original *Goodbye Mr. Chips* on television. In this, Robert Donat, leading a dull life as a teacher in an English prepa-ratory school, meets Greer Garson on a walking tour of the Alps, and his life is forever changed. Martin later felt that this film had affected his decision.)

Walking alone for three weeks, he began to feel that his life was somehow empty, that something important was missing. Walking all day in the crisp springtime air of Vermont and New Hampshire, he felt at once exhila-rated and depressed. He began to realize that he badly needed something new, but could form no idea of what it might be.

What he did not realize at the time was that he was beginning to go through what Jung has called "the second adolescence." From Jung's viewpoint, those who are for-tunate enough to go through this process generally do so between 35 and 65. During the process, those who succeed in the developmental task of this period find their major interests shifting from concern with things and with the opinions of others to concern with the growth of the self. On his return to the city, he made an appointment for psychotherapy.

In the first sessions he made it plain that he had little hope for anything new for him in life and that he was largely going through the motions, but doing this so expertly that everyone around him believed him to be a real success in life. He had little or no psychic pain and indeed seemed to have little involvement with himself or with anything else.

What seemed to be needed was an essentially psycho-analytic approach. He had to learn again to use his excellent mind by using it. The ideal method for getting in touch with his abilities was to use these abilities to explore himself. He needed to be put to work in a disciplined manner on a tough problem in order to relearn that he really existed and could solve tough problems. And to find that he would enjoy this. Indeed, among the first things he discovered was that he was a person who enjoyed learning new things, but he had forgotten this and had fed his mind no new nourishment for a long time. Because of his interest in business management, he began to read (and to audit some courses in his college and in a nearby university) about the history of that field and its relation to other aspects of cultural development. In two years or so he found to his surprise that he was teaching several new courses, had published three papers on the subject, and had something of a reputation as an expert in it.

The procedure that probably would have fit him the best was a psychoanalytic approach, although only twice a week and not using a couch. Through free association, dream analysis, and exploration of the transference, he was led quickly to his fear of deep relationships and, indeed, of being deeply committed to anything. His relationship with his daughter improved markedly as did that with one of the two women with whom he had been having a long-term affair. They are now living together, and both see it as "a probably permanent" arrangement. He finds a great deal of satisfaction in working two evenings a week as the volunteer business manager of an ecology organization.

He now seems to be so committed to and engaged in his life that he does not ask whether he is enjoying it: he *knows* its meaning and value. He says with a laugh, "I wonder what my next walking trip will lead to."

Patient 4: Harvey

Harvey's father was a very successful restaurant owner and bon vivant. Wherever he was, he held the center of the floor. When he was not there, Mother, an ex-actress, held it. He married a dominating, highly verbal, emotional woman and left all decisions to her. There were four children who all followed the mother in verbal and emotional style. Harvey loved them and was an excellent if rather silent father. He was very good with his hands and enjoyed very much (or, rather, would have enjoyed very much) fixing things around the house. However, early in the marriage his wife made it plain that when things needed to be done in the house, professionals were better than amateurs, and professionals were always called in.

This is the first patient I have ever had who bored me. He was in charge of window dressing for a chain of inexpensive department stores. I know more about this subject than I ever wished to. No matter what I did, no matter what subjects I brought up, we mainly talked about the art and science of window dressing. Halfway through each session, my eyes began to glaze. Soon I began to dread the sessions with him.

I discussed this with my control therapist Anne Appelbaum. She listened, asked some questions, and said, "He comes to see you all the way from Brooklyn, and that is a long hard trip. He sets the subject and pace. Obviously you are missing something that is very important to him. *He is not there to amuse you*! Let's find out why you are blocking on what he *is* there for."

I began to ask myself what this particular person needed in order to grow and become. He did not seem to want or need a warm or close relationship. He did seem to do best when I just paid attention to him, listened to him, and (now that I stopped feeling any inner pressure to "*do* something"—this was easy to do) liked him.

But things began to change with him at home, and, in the few minutes every session or two that we talked about this (instead of about window dressing), I began to be aware of it. New electrical wiring was needed in the kitchen at home. He had a blazing row with his wife (the first they had ever had) over who would do this. He went out and bought a set of carpenter tools he had wanted for many years and did the work. Since then he has built a deck behind the house and a new set of front steps. When I last saw him, he was beginning to replace the window frames on evenings and weekends and enjoying it immensely. He and his wife had always wanted to go to Morocco. One day he came home and told her he had arranged with a travel agent that they would go there for their next vacation. She was amazed and found herself very pleased to let him make all the arrangements—a job she had done for all their previous trips. Since then they have traveled to Africa several times, with his making the arrangements. His wife told me that she felt their marriage was vastly improved, and he agreed. A quite malignant tumor that was present when he first came to see me has responded beautifully to treatment and is now "indolent," present but not growing.

The therapeutic environment that Harvey needed was a cool, friendly one in which he was, possibly for the first time in his life, listened to and paid attention to. In it, he flourished.

Harvey reminds me of a rather similar situation that occurred in the late 1940s. I was at the University of Chicago and working part-time in the clinic where Carl Rogers was experimenting with what he called "nondirective therapy." (Being a grown-up, Rogers soon gave this up.) In the clinic we all considered it to be the "right" way to do therapy and were trying hard to learn it and do it in an absolutely orthodox manner.

One graduate student, Chuck Wharton, was assigned a client. The man came in, said hello, and went right to the couch that was in the office (probably left over from an earlier psychoanalytically oriented period) and lay down on it. He said nothing for the next hour, and so, following the rules of nondirective therapy, Wharton said nothing either. At the end of the hour, the patient stood up, said, "Thank you, see you Thursday," and left. Wharton was very upset and brought the problem up at the staff meeting the next day. Rogers asked about the client's demeanor, looked at the social work intake report, and told Wharton, "Wait." Wharton said, "I'll try."

For the next two and a half months, twice a week, the client came in, said hello to Wharton and lay down silently on the couch for the hour. Wharton's anxiety level kept mounting, but each time he brought the matter up, Rogers said, "He keeps coming. His greetings are friendly. Wait."

At the end of the two and a half months, the client suddenly sat up in the middle of a ·session and said, "Thank you, Mr. Wharton. You are the first person who ever believed that I had the ability to solve my own problems. I have learned here exactly what I have to do and am now ready to do it. This has been the single most rewarding experience of my life."

And left.

The environment that this patient needed was clearly different from that of many others. The therapy was successful because by coincidence *what was needed by this person and what was offered by the therapist were the same. When that coincidence happens, our therapies are successful. When they are not the same, they are not successful.*

Even if you fail in understanding the patient well enough to design the correct environment for him, the fact that you cared enough to try, and that you responded to him as an individual, is communicated and has a positive effect. Similarly, when we are not treating the person as an individual person but only as a member of the species "patient," this is communicated with a negative effect.

It takes time to know what a patient needs. We do not learn this in the first session, but slowly. The first session is like opening a novel of Tolstoy or Dostoyevsky and reading the first page. We know the protagonist's name, sex, present setting, and a bit more. Each session is another page or, if you are experienced, another chapter. Slowly we get to know who this patient is and what his world of existence is like. Slowly one understands more and more of what he needs to grow and flourish in his own way.

But we will never know unless the question is salient and clear to us. Unless our attitude is that of the gardener saying, "This patient has strong needs to grow in his or her unique direction. What special environment, including the therapist, is needed?"

Not only do we have much to learn about the different environments needed for our patients to best move forward on their paths; it is also very hard for us psychotherapists to accept the fact that the same approach is not valid for all of them. The psychiatrist Herbert Spiegel, for example, has been trying for many years to point this out to his colleagues, with little success in spite of the fact that he writes cogently and expertly and has published widely on this subject. (See Spiegel 1974, Spiegel and Greenleaf 1992, Spiegel and Shainess 1963, Spiegel and Spiegel 1978.)

Spiegel has devised a specialized instrument for looking at different patients' different needs for psychotherapy approaches, techniques of stress management, crisis intervention, and so forth. He calls this "the fix-flex continuum," and it describes the degree to which the patient is oriented to inner or to outer cues, his "ecological sensitivity and insensitivity." This is the most advanced single instrument that we have for this, but it is only a beginning.

Spiegel and psychologist Marcia Greenleaf (1992) do much crisis intervention and use a good deal of hypnosis in their work. Before the intervention each patient is interviewed in depth, and the intervention is then designed specifically and individually for each patient. Their results are far better than those of anyone else I know of because they design their interventions around the patient's needs rather than using a generalized approach.

We are learning, as we move into the next developmental phase of psychotherapy, that not only must our methods and relationships be different with each patient but also that we must be very careful of our models and metaphors. Science uses them widely, but they always promise more than they can deliver and almost always backfire. They almost invariably cost us more understanding than they give us. We have had to learn, for example, that an atom is not a small solar system; that civilization is not a plant that grows, flowers, withers, and dies; and that a human being does not fit any model yet made. We can describe Albert Einstein, Al Capone, and Albert Schweitzer with many models. We can use Freud's hydraulic pump, Carlyle's steam engine, a white rat writ large, a flowering plant, a computer, a partially tamed carnivore, a Libra, a first born, or what have you. All leave much out. All present only flat and one-dimensional pictures. If we use only one model or any one model, we lose the richness, the individuality, the specialness, the humanness of the person. The color goes out. It is all monochromatic.

In his Hibbert lectures in 1908, William James described how we commonly make metaphors for human beings, lose the human being in them, and defend them with experiment and logic.

We proceed, he said, by first singling out some concrete thing or aspect and excluding the rest of what it means to be human. We then identify the concrete aspect with the whole person. We then demonstrate, through logic or experiment, that, looked at in this way, the person does not include any other aspects.

For example, we use (as did many psychologists for many years) as a metaphor a white rat. We design experiments that deal with ratlike characteristics and then, since our experiments demonstrate these characteristics, say that we have proven that human beings are white rats writ large.

Or, as did many therapists, we take the concept of Hobbes and Freud as to the basic nature of human beings, and this strongly influences our view of how to work in therapy. We may or may not have verbalized this viewpoint, but its influence can be very strong. (For a more detailed discussion of this point, see Appendix I.)

Once we have fully accepted a metaphor for human beings, we simply block out any evidence that it does not encompass the *entire* human being. Or else we force the evidence into the Procustean bed of our metaphor. Our science then becomes, in Karl Popper's words, "nonfalsifiable"—there is no possibility of it being proven wrong. We are then no longer scientists but zealots. If you do not comprehend this, ask a devoted Marxist, Astrologer, Psychoanalyst, or Humanistic-Psychologist to tell you of a hypothetical crucial experiment or experience in their field—something that would prove that their basic assumptions were not correct. If they cannot do this, their science is (at best) a pseudo-science since it is nonfalsifiable.

Indeed, the oldest metaphor we have for human beings or for the human mind is just as good, and just as useless, as that of the most modern computer. The newest one and most "in" one changes from day to day. The oldest of which we have a record is Plato's metaphor of the mind as a charioteer who has to control two very different horses at the same time. These are the horse of reason and the horse of emotion. This metaphor has no particular advantage over or disadvantage to the more modern ones listed earlier.

By and large, we tend to be so convinced of the basic truth of the metaphors and concepts and methods that we were taught in our training that we simply do not observe when a patient does not fit them or benefit by them and do not draw any conclusions from this.

In the old Zen story, the man came to the Zen Master in search of wisdom. The Master consented to teach him but said that first he would give him some tea. Into the student's cup he poured tea until it was full to the brim and then kept pouring so that the tea from the pot overflowed the cup and spilled down to the floor. The student asked why he was doing this. The Zen Master replied that the student's mind was so filled with his ideas about reality that he was unable to learn anything new and that until he first emptied out some of his ideas by questioning them, he could learn nothing new. The filled teacup represented the filled mind and the uselessness of trying to put anything new in it. In Robert Heinlein's (1985) words:

> The hardest part about gaining any new ideas is sweeping out the false ideas occupying that niche. So long as the niche is occupied evidence, proof and logical demonstration get nowhere. [p. 230]

There is a general unfortunate tendency for each of us to compartmentalize and treat as important about other persons what we are especially trained to see and to ignore the rest. Specialization in medicine has progressed to the point where everyone knows the jokes about the physician who treats only the *left* nostril. (There are thirty-seven separate board specializations in medicine today, and it is undoubtedly just a coincidence that there were the same number in Egyptian medicine at the time of Cleopatra!) Psychologists tend to ignore the whole person in front of them and only treat the psychological problems for which they were trained. This is unfortunate for the patient, but common. We all know the oncologist who acts as if a group of cells has come into his or her office and is to be treated rather than a person. (They tend, in my experience, to be the worst offenders in this regard. However, I do know a very good cardiologist who dismisses one of his patient's severe abdominal pain and acts as if it does not exist since it is, in his expert opinion, unrelated to the heart problems he is so successfully treating.) For psychotherapists to ignore the physical and the spiritual aspects of their patients is to focus our work so narrowly that we are almost certain to be, at best, curing rather than healing.

The tendency, however, to do this, to see our fellow humans as only one aspect, the one we are interested in at the moment, or trained or oriented to see, is very strong. As Thomas Arnold, Headmaster of Rugby, wrote before 1850:

> As man sets up a factory and *wants hands*, I beseech you, sir, to observe the very expressions that are used, for they are all significant. What he wants of his fellow creatures is the loan of their hands; of their heads and hearts he thinks nothing. [quoted in Heilbroner 1959, p. 37]

It is not, of course, only psychotherapy that has suffered from the human need to narrow and simplify matters and to explain everything with one system. Marxists, astrologers, economists, and a wide variety of others are just as bad as orthodox psychoanalysts, behaviorists, existentialists, or other single-trackers in

the psychological field. The spiritual directors of organized religion also frequently have fallen prey to this.
Thomas Merton (1961) points out that many spiritual
directors have found their system "infallible in all cases"
and completely ignored individual differences and individual circumstances. "Others," he says sadly, used
their system to "take satisfaction in indulging their aggressive instincts" (p. 18).

In Appendix II, I discuss in detail the tendency we
have had in psychology to make metaphors for human
beings and to lose the human beings in the process.

————·◆·————

.The ancient Greeks, in their medical and political
theories, used two words to describe collections of
things. The first, *mixis*, indicated a collection of things
that just were together—for example, cars in a parking
lot, plates on a shelf, pebbles lying near each other on
a path. The second, *krasis*, indicated a collection of different elements that positively affect and support each
other—for example, the alloy bronze made up of cop-
per and tin. Bronze is far stronger and far more able to
hold an edge than either of the other two. It indicates a
unity that is far more than a mixture. A crowd is a *mixis*;
a football team is a *krasis*.

As part of the healing process, our task is to redefine our lives so that our activities—mental, spiritual,
and physical—form a *krasis*, not a *mixis*, a mixture
where each part supports the others. Clement of Alex-
andria in the fourth century described this by saying,
"All parts of the being breathe together." He went on to
say that it was this concept that made the Roman army
so powerful. For the deliberate and conscious selection
of parts so that they would make a greater whole, the
Greeks used the word *s'ya-krasis*.

In therapy, we try to redefine our lives and help a patient with whom we are working redefine his life so that all the parts relate to and support and strengthen the other parts. We try to unify the person so that they act as a coherent whole that becomes more than the sum of the parts and that has greater effectiveness than the parts.

————•◆•————

Each metaphor makes the person into something of a "nothing but." Each of us is always more, and to forget this is to do violence to the person.

So the therapist teaches the patients to listen to, care, hope for, and respect themselves by modeling this, by doing it in action. But there is more. As the therapist and part of the environment, we also model in how we live our own lives. Do we listen to, care for, hope for, and respect ourselves enough to spend as much time, thought, energy, and action on ourselves as we do on our most difficult and loved patient? If not, aren't we saying, "Do as I say, not as I do"? And, don't we all remember how flat and uninspiring this statement is? Or else, perhaps, we are saying, "I don't believe in this stuff, but I am telling you to do it anyway." Or, even worse, "I have arrived and am completely mature" or "I have been completely analyzed and am a clear, or enlightened, or what not, but you, you poor. . . ."

There was a wonderful child psychiatrist, Fritz Redl, who died a few years ago. His book *Children Who Hate* is still a great classic. Shortly after World War II he was lecturing to a group of parents of young children. One of them asked, "Dr. Redl, in times like these when everyone seems corrupt, when politicians and baseball players and everyone else the children look up to are so corrupt, how can we bring our children up so that they will live as adults of good character?" Redl replied, "There are three things you must do to accomplish this. I want you to write them down." Everyone in the audience, including myself, got our paper and pens ready. Then Redl said, "The three things are, example, example, example!"

How do you work at your own growth? I do not mean only reading material (even if it is as outstanding as this is!) but actual work, as in a gymnasium?

What part of you has been the least watered, nourished, cared for during the last period of your life? Do you plan to do something about this?

Are you losing your zest as a therapist? Is the work becoming routine, boring? Do you find yourself repeating the same things over and over? Have you stopped growing and changing?

By and large is each five-year period of your life more full of zest and fun than the previous periods? If not, should you consider stopping being a psychotherapist since you are giving your patients the message "There is a limit to growth"? Are you greedy for more experience and of your life? If not, how can you make your patients greedy?

This is one of the reasons that we need constant supervision. It is not only that there will always be patients who will press buttons in us that we did not know were there. It is not only that we will always have unexamined and unlived-out areas in us that make us blind to certain aspects of our patients' problems. It is that it is necessary for us to keep growing and changing and that working with another person on this is a major way that we have chosen by the very nature of being in this profession.

The need for supervision does not change with age and experience. The finest therapist I have ever known (to whom this book is dedicated) is now 86, still in practice, and she is still working with a control therapist.

Each profession makes its own demands. The athlete needs to keep his or her total body tuned and trained. The therapist needs to keep on growing and changing and developing. He or she needs to keep a constant weather eye on their own becoming.

In the last five years, as a therapist have you had five years of experience or one year of experience repeated five times? Is there a paper you wrote five years ago that you do not wish you could recall and rewrite? Is there a patient you had five years ago that you could not do better with now? If not, what are you saying about your own growth and your ability to model growth for your patients?

Not only do we need supervision on a fairly regular basis for as long as we are in practice, we must also know our craft. It takes long study of the human condition, knowledge of the research and experience in our field, as well as a good deal of personal therapy. Hopefully this personal therapy will be with therapists from different schools. This is the best way to learn that while all schools have validity in certain areas of the human experience, none have exclusive rights to the whole territory. Although one model and method may be valid for our growth at certain times as we follow our path, none has a monopoly—all systems limp.

As we, on the basis of nearly a hundred years of experience, begin to redesign psychotherapy for the twenty-first century, we are beginning to see it as the creation of a special environment specifically designed for the patient to grow in his or her own way, pacing, and style, in order to become more and more themselves, not more and more adjusted to reality as defined by the local cultural milieu. We are beginning to see what *respect* for the patient really implies. That what is important is not what the therapist does for or to the patient but what the therapist creates and keeps creating—an environment for growth.

We are just beginning to learn how to do this—how to determine what each individual patient needs in order to thrive and grow toward his or her uniqueness. There is a very great deal about this which we do not yet know. However, as long as we are trying to do this, as long as the idea is salient to us, this is communicated to patients. If we listen to them, they will help us learn.

The fact of our "trying" is, in itself, helpful. As an adolescent, my daughter, Wendy, was once asked how it felt to be raised by two psychologists. She said, "Oh, they made the same mistakes as everybody else, but I always knew that they were trying."

This is a change of a basic assumption in the field. We were taught and believed that there were things we could do to and for the patient that would heal him. This has very strongly influenced us and our work. Most of us felt that, before a patient came into our consulting room for the first time, we knew generally what model we would use and what we would strive to do. We would, we knew, try to bring the unconscious material to consciousness, or assuage neurotic guilt over childhood affairs, or teach social skills, or put him in touch with his inner child, or teach him to accept his whatever, or follow other definite paths and seek other special previously defined, if often never verbalized, goals.

This was comfortable, eased our doubts, and fed our narcissism (after all, we *knew* what was best for this person), and it worked. It worked just often enough to keep us going. It worked when *by coincidence* the patient's needs and the model and method we used fit together. When these two came together, the patient was able to heal—to grow in his or her own way, to become.

Sometimes even when this was not true, we could cure the specific problems of the patient. The very fact of the patient's having made a serious effort to take control of his life through going into therapy could be helpful in the increased sense of confidence in himself that it gave him. Sometimes the therapy provided a new explanation of problems, a new story into which to fit his life that could make it possible to function without specific symptoms. After all, as Viktor Frankl used to remark, the facts, including the facts of our interior life, are far less important than our attitude toward them. (The world, said the poet Muriel Rukeyser, its made up of stories, not of atoms.) Sometimes the new rationalization provided by the model of the therapist changed the attitude of the patient toward certain facts and thereby removed the symptom. There are other reasons we sometimes *cure*, often reasons we are completely unaware of.

This is perhaps illustrated by an incident that happened to the psychiatrist John Rosen. He was a specialist in dealing with severely disturbed patients and understanding the nature of their fantasy life and, by this understanding, helping to lead them to abandon its self-destructive components. A man he had seen on consultation in a mental hospital's locked ward escaped and developed an obsession that Rosen was persecuting him. One day he burst into Rosen's office and, drawing a knife, placed it against Rosen's throat and said that because of the persecution, he was going to kill him. Rosen realized that it would not be possible to talk the man out of his obsession and decided to use his training in understanding the fantasies of schizophrenics to try to save himself. He said, "You don't want to put that knife into my throat. You want to put your penis into my mouth." The man looked at him with horror, dropped the knife on the floor, and ran away. Later he was picked up by the police, whom Rosen had immediately called, and was asked why he had run away. He replied, "When he said that, I realized that he was completely crazy and that if I had anything more to do with him, I might become as crazy as he was!"

There is indeed a very high demand that this new development of psychotherapy makes on the members of our profession. It says that the long and hard work that we each have done learning how to *do* psychotherapy and our devotion to our patients is not enough. It says that we must also learn, if we wish to be therapists who heal and not only mechanics who fix and cure, other models and methods and ways of relating and shift according to the patient's needs. And that, when a patient needs a model, method, and environment that we are not at ease and expert with, we should refer that person to another therapist who is.

Further, it says that our teachers and mentors were wrong when they said that what they were teaching you was the right way to do therapy. This is hard to accept as these are people we revere and respect. But they and we are creatures of our time, and a new era is arriving. Human beings are provincial in time as well as in space, and a new time is at hand.

Indeed, so high is the demand, that if the majority of psychotherapists reading this do not feel some resentment and anger toward me, I have, perhaps, not been specific enough.

Our new view is that we can only teach patients to respect themselves by our respecting them and that this means our having respect for their ability to grow and flourish in their own way and direction if we provide a proper garden, a correct environment for them to do this. We are not, working in this way, fixing or curing but going back to our ancient roots. We are going back to being *healers* again.

2

CURING AND
HEALING

Abe Maslow used to say in his lectures, "To oversimplify the matter, it is as if Freud supplied to us the sick half of psychology and we must now fill it out with the healthy half." In terms of the psychological aspects of human beings, Freud taught us how to *cure*, probably the greatest single boon any individual ever gave us. Now, moving into the second century of psychotherapy, we are learning how to *heal*. Curing helps with a particular problem. Healing sets in process an orientation toward the self that will help the individual solve the many future problems that will arise as long as the person lives.

To cure means to focus on a particular problem and to use appropriate techniques. To heal means to provide an environment for the patient to grow in, in which to thrive so that he will be able to better handle future

problems on his own. The twin keys to helping the patient realize that he can use his own abilities to solve
his problems and to help him learn to use them in his
own way are respect and caring. To be effective, these
must be expressed in action, not only in words.

> Jewish tradition has long recognized that there are two
> components of health: the body and the spirit. The *Mi
> Sheberach* prayer, traditionally recited for someone who
> is ill, asks God for *refuah shlema,* a complete healing,
> and then specifies two aspects: *refuah hanefesh,* heal-
> ing of the soul/spirit/whole person, and *refuah haguf,*
> cure of the body. To cure the body means to wipe out
> the tumor, clear up the infection, or regain mobility. To
> heal the spirit, involves creating a pathway to sensing
> wholeness, depth, mystery, purpose, and peace.
>   Cure may occur without healing, and healing with-
> out cure. Pastoral caregivers and family members of
> seriously ill people know that sometimes lives and re-
> lationships are healed even when there is no possibil-
> ity of physical cure; in fact, serious illness often moti-
> vates people to seek healing of the spirit. [Flam 1994,
> p. 36]

The distinction between our "curing" and "healing"
functions as psychotherapists has become very blurred.
This condition has seriously decreased our ability to
help our patients in any way. If, during the therapy
process, the therapist is not aware of what he or she is
trying to do, what in the world can we expect of our
results?

It is essential that the therapist keep the therapeutic goal in mind and that the process be relevant to it.
Certainly they may overlap. I may concentrate on curing a particular pain or function loss so that the patient
may be free to grow and become. I may, conversely,

concentrate on a patient's becoming in the hope that this will stimulate her immune system and thereby help cure a particular physical illness. But I will do these things far better if I am aware of what I am trying to do.

When working with people with severe illness, the health care professional has three tasks: to cure where possible, to alleviate where it is not, and to give safe passage. When working with people who are not facing life-threatening stressors, the psychotherapist's task entails at least certainly the first two. We try to help the patient cure specific problems where we can and to alleviate the pain of these where this is all we can do. This is the real and valid part of our work that comes from our inheritance from the medical profession and model. However, the other real and valid part of our tradition—the part that comes from the wise men and women of the community—leaves us with a different inheritance and a different task. This is to heal, to help patients reorient themselves and their view of their being and their relationships that they lead fuller and richer lives and are more able to solve specific problems themselves. It is important that the therapist is aware of what he or she is trying to do and further that therapist and patient are in agreement about the goals of their work. If not in agreement, at the very least, they should be aware of their own goals and those of the other person involved.

In the healing environment, whatever this might be for any individual person, all parts of the individual ultimately come to the fore and are seen as integral. No one single factor or specific goal is sufficient; the person must be seen as a whole with all parts of importance. It is not just being expressive or angry or thin or able to jog seven miles a day or being in touch with your inner child that promotes healing, although any of these may be, with the relevant patient, able to help cure specific problems. The whole person must be ultimately dealt with.

When, for example, the spiritual is neglected (as it has been in most psychotherapies of the twentieth century), it does not just go away. It reappears in the prevention of healing even though more specific problems may have been cured. Neglecting it prevents the invigoration of the healing orientation and process whereby future problems may be helped to be cured. And the individual helped to go forward on his or her own, individual path through life.

It sometimes happens that our techniques (for a reason we do not comprehend) cure the patient of the specific problem he has brought to us, the problem that triggered his coming to therapy. We then confidently expect that he will go on and upgrade his life in other areas, but to our chagrin and surprise, this does not happen. We have "cured" him, but no real healing process has gotten under way. In these cases what has apparently happened is that we were unaware of what environment the patient needed in order to grow. The lack of further progress in moving toward a life of zest and enthusiasm should serve as a signal to us that it is now necessary to reevaluate the situation, find the optimum environment for this person's flourishing, and either provide it or refer him to someone who can.

Z. was a successful businessman who sold his company and retired at the age of 50. He was thoroughly bored with his present life, rather depressed, and dissatisfied with his marriage. There was little relationship with his daughter. The presenting problem was a malignant melanoma that was being treated with one of the serious alternative approaches. The psychotherapeutic strategy used was discussion of his feelings in a warm, respectful environment in which he knew that he was liked and appreciated as a person. The stress was on finding new sources of using his marked creative energies now that the cathexis of business work, which he had much enjoyed and worked very hard at, was now closed. There was discussion of his childhood experiences and how they had led to the present situation. These were primarily intellectual, with not very much emotional activity. His cancer responded exceptionally well to the treatment he was receiving and was no longer present to observation. However, there was no change in the general gray quality of his life and the overall picture of boredom.

What this man needed as an environment in which he could flourish was one that would have made him work as hard as he ever had while in business. Ideally he would have been in a situation in which he knew that he was approved of. There should have been something like art therapy in which he had to interpret his own drawings or free association and dream analysis with very little interpretation by the therapist. The Associative Amanuensis of Felix Deutsch, with its very hard and constant pressure, might also have been applicable. A modern but reasonably orthodox Freudian, Jungian, or Adlerian approach, once or twice a week with warmth but very little interpretation, might have been very effective. Another possibility might have been a bioenergetic approach as, for example, practiced and taught by Stanley Keleman.

However, I did not realize this at the time. The original approach was continued in spite of the lack of progress after the presenting symptom had been dealt with with apparent success. After another year, which we both agreed was a fruitless one, the therapy was abandoned.

———— •◆• ————

In terms of our setting up an "ecological niche" in which patients can grow rather than our "growing them up," we have learned (alas!), often through hard and bitter experience, that we cannot rescue anyone who needs and wants rescuing. No matter how often we therapists, from motives of love and caring mixed with a soupçon of deep faith in the power of our methods, rescue a particular patient, we find that at best we have applied a temporary balm and Band-Aid to a deep and suppurating wound. The pattern soon repeats. Not until we have taught a patient how *and why* to rescue himself does the wound and the person begin to heal.

The "why" is clearly at least as important as the "how" (if not more so). The patient must, partially through our modeling, first learn to see himself as really worthy of rescue before he really can act in favor of his own growth and protection. Only then does the "repetition compulsion," or whatever else we call the tendency to get himself in the same mess over and over again, cease to control his life.

It is important for us to keep in mind the old fable about the two missionaries. The first, you remember, full of love and compassion, fished for the poor, benighted, starving natives and fed them. The second, with a hard heart and clear mind, taught them to fish for themselves!

The therapist must keep in mind the real goal: to make him- or herself obsolete. Immanuel Kant wrote, "You will learn from me not philosophy, but to philosophise, not thoughts, but to think" (quoted in Rank 1948, p. 1). If the therapist is clear that the end product of the work with patients is to enable them to live as fully and richly as possible and to have their own adventures in their own style, the whole proceeding takes on a different tone.

The basic tendency of therapists to be oriented to helping their patients adjust rather than become, conform and be comfortable rather than individual, is much more widespread and pernicious than is usually believed. As acute an observer as Bertrand Russell wrote:

> I have been struck especially in America, by . . . the passion of psychiatrists and psychoanalysts for making their patients ordinary. I have had in America arguments with psychiatrists employed at military hospitals in the course of which they explicitly maintained that any person who is in any degree in conflict with the herd is in need of psychological treatment. When I said, "How about Christ and Galileo?" they would imply, though they hardly dared to say definitely, that they hoped no such subversive persons would turn up in the United States. [Lindner 1953, back cover]

The ideas expressed in this book are certainly not original with the author. Otto Rank, for example, wrote in 1929 that the goal of psychotherapy should be:

> self-development, that is the person is to develop himself into that which he is and not, as in education and even in psychoanalytic therapy, to be made into a good citizen who accepts the general ideals without contradiction and has no will of his own. [p. 228]

———•◆•———

An old and well-known concept in psychotherapy is that of "the therapeutic alliance." In this the therapist and the best part of the patient feel themselves allied in the search for the best, the thriving, of the whole patient. How is this made? What must the therapist *do* to ensure the alliance comes into being?

There is, of course, nothing specific for the therapist to *do*. If there were, it would imply a one-size-fits-all gimmick and be absolutely opposed to the entire philosophy of this book. What is needed is an *attitude* on the part of the therapist—an attitude of respect for the best (the efforts, dreams, hopes, growth) of the patient and acceptance of these: a sense that the healthy parts of the patient are already searching for better ways of being, relating, creating, and it is part of the therapist's task to work together with these. Nothing specific needs to be done, but if this attitude is present, it will influence and help shape the therapist's words, actions, and body language. The patient *will* be aware of it.

A story about Freda Fromm-Reichmann illustrates one way this happened in a specific situation (M. Gassmann, personal communication, 1960). She had been the therapist described in the well-known book *I Never Promised You a Rose Garden*. Some years after publication, she met the author who had been her patient. Fromm-Reichmann said to her, "What *really* cured you?" The author replied, "It was the first sentence you said to me. After that I knew I would be alright." Fromm-Reichmann asked what that sentence had been and received the reply that it was "What are *we* going to do about you?" The ex-patient went on to say that this was the first time anyone had ever included her as a full partner in the situation.

It should be unnecessary to repeat that this sentence has no magical universal qualities. Unless it grows organically out of the situation, unless it comes trippingly on the tongue, it is a gimmick and phony and will not have really beneficial effects. It is a violation of Miale's Law:

> It is the relationship that heals. [And that] is the single most important lesson the psychotherapist must learn. There is no more self-evident truth in psychotherapy; every therapist observes over and over in clinical work that the encounter itself is healing for the patient in a

way that transcends the therapist's theoretical orientation. [Yalom, quoted in Willis 1994, p. 109]

———————•◆•———————

Among the sacred cows that most of us were raised on in our professional training was the idea that there is something especially meritorious about the experimental method and particularly about statistics, something that gives them the final say in our disputes. It is not so much that we *actually* change our minds about important matters very often when experiment or statistical study proves us wrong. In actuality, we tend to remember the studies that agree with our previous positions and forget those that disagree. However, we feel we *ought* to change our minds because of them and our opponents certainly should when the study gives results we agree with. Our opponents don't, which simply proves their pigheadedness.

So far as individual examples go, if they disagree with our point of view, we feel quite free to dismiss them as "anecdotal evidence." If they agree with our position, then, of course, they are "case reports" and are regarded as important.

However much or little the statistical reports may be helpful, with the tremendous variation among human beings, once you get to be concerned with anything more important than how many combinations of a puff of air and a bell it takes to establish a conditioned response eye-blink to the bell, the statistics tell you absolutely nothing about the person in front of you. Until you carefully check it out, you cannot be certain that the individual with whom you are dealing is not William James's "one white crow" that proves all crows are not black. Alfred Korzybski used to say that the only generalizations you could depend on were negative ones of the sort "All children of any class of parents are not heterosexual," "All people with stomach ulcers do not have unusually large amounts of unexpressed dependency needs," "All chairs are not made of wood," or "All alcoholics did not have alcoholic or abusive parents." Beyond this kind of statement, there is absolutely nothing that statistical or experimental studies can tell you about the patient in front of you. Or, as my old teacher, the psychiatrist Abraham Meyerson, used to say:

> As soon as you have decided, on the basis of long experience and sound theory, that all patients who have "A" also have "B," within three days some character will come into your office with "A" but without "B." The big question is not whether or not this will happen—it will—but whether or not you will notice it!

It is not only the specific facts and correlations of facts of which we are so certain and that may or may not apply to this specific patient. It is also the general theory and system that we use to perceive the total situation. It is difficult to keep in mind that we have been taught and have well learned an overall philosophy, a system of thought that may or may not apply. Some systems are extremely convenient for our work as psychotherapists, but we have none yet that can validate a claim to universal truth. The metaphor most useful for one patient is not most useful for others. Not everyone who comes into our office has lost contact with their inner child or is fixated at an early stage of development. As Marcia Greenleaf, a health psychologist, teaches hospital personnel, some patients before major surgery benefit by discussing their feelings openly; some do not and may even be more disturbed and made more anxious by doing this. Sometimes a spouse needs to discuss the problems and sometimes not. Sometimes patient and spouse (or "important other") need to be open with each other; sometimes it is more anxiety producing if they are. The basic rule is definitely not "What's sauce for the goose is sauce for the gander" but rather, as Hippocrates pointed out so many years ago (in different words), "One man's meat is another man's poison."

The anthropologist Clifford Geertz (1983) has pointed out that it is not only psychotherapists who believe that their world view is the correct way and that the correct way to live within this is the one they know. It is also most of the people that the psychotherapists respect and have learned from:

> The only thing that links Freud, Piaget, von Neumann, and Chomsky (to say nothing of Jung and B.F. Skinner) is their conviction that the mechanics of human thinking is [sic] immutable across time, space, culture, and circumstance and that they know what it is. [p. 150]

Systems are useful tools but bad masters. Bertrand Russell (1929) said, "Regarded merely as hypotheses and as aids to the imagination, the great systems of the past serve a useful purpose" (p. vii). Similarly, the great systems of the present also do, including our present favorite.

In terms of this, we now come to what is probably the single hardest thing for an experienced or inexperienced psychotherapist to remember. Yet it is probably the most important thing. This is how little we know for certain about our subject and the surety that half of what we are now sure of will be regarded by future generations as extremely inadequate metaphor at best and most likely as primitive thinking on our part. The only trouble is that what we do not know about any particular idea or bit of what we regard as "knowledge" is into which half it belongs—the half that will be discarded or the half that will be retained.

If you think that this is an exaggeration—the idea that at least one half of the things you deeply believe about human behavior will not be believed a hundred years hence—then look backward. No theory of any science deeply believed in as "final" in 1865 was accepted as true in that form in 1965. (I choose 1965 as the place to start as many of you or your teachers were getting your education and forming your scientific prejudices about that time.) Do you really believe that the development of science and knowledge in your field has slowed up so much that things are different now? If you do, you are wrong. Matters are quite the other way around. It is true that you could legitimately describe the scientific endeavor as a systematic attempt to establish closed and complete systems one after the other. It is the last phrase that is the problem. As soon (or shortly after) as a complete system of explanation is devised, someone comes along and shows it is incomplete. This happened with Newton, and it happened with Freud. Tempting as they are to us, the universe and the human mind are simply not up for complete explanations. If you really believe that your system of explanation really explains everything important about your patients, you probably feel pretty comfortable. However, you are fooling yourself by leaving out large parts of your patients. And you are certainly not doing them as much good as you think. (How would *you* thrive if your therapist ignored major aspects of your being?) Santayana (1891) put this in his usual style:

> Those who deal with the abstract and general, who think impersonally and along the lines of a universal system,

are almost sure to ignore their own ignorance. They acquire what has been called the architectonic instinct; their conception of things is bound to be symmetrical and balanced, and to fit into one another with perfect precision. . . .

Their cold breath congeals the surface of truths and on that thin ice they glide merrily over all the chasms in their knowledge. [pp. 555–556]

Writes Jacob Bronowski (1978):

There is no system of axioms which can embrace the whole of nature, or for that matter, the whole of mathematics. . . . we will never be able to exhibit the whole of physics one fine day as a gorgeous system with about six axioms and a few operations, and from that moment everything would fall into place. . . . Anything you could ask would follow from the axiomatic system. [p. 80]

Bronowski is writing of physics and mathematics. What he says is as true of psychology. We look for a total system of explanation for human thought and behavior. Each time we think we have one it turns out to be inadequate and partial at best. Psychoanalysis explains some things and not others. The same is true of Behaviorism and any other system you find or devise. The universe and human beings are simply too complex for any one system of evaluation. We all find this very disappointing.

As Bronowski said:

The society of scientists, the community of scientists, has this advantage, that from the moment we enter it, we all know that fifty years from now, most of the things we learned here will turn out not to have been quite right. [p. 130]

If only we could teach this to the students training to be psychotherapists! If only we could teach it saying, "The methods and metaphors I teach you here are the best I know at this moment. If you listen to your patients, they will teach you more. They will lead you to new methods and metaphors. They will show you the limitations of my approach and how to go beyond it. Then you will teach what you know to your students, and, if you teach well, they will go beyond you."

Unfortunately, it sometimes happens in our field that a group of students accept a system and model as divine revelation and go on, year after year, decade after decade, frozen into the same method. Tiny changes may be made (professional papers are written on miniscule points), but the basic doctrine and technique remain unchanged. A few days ago I spoke to two patients who were in formal psychoanalysis with the same analyst. She had been on the couch five days a week for five years. He could, because of job difficulties, come only four days a week. He had just started six months before and had been told that he should expect to continue for six to ten years.

I felt as if I had just opened a time capsule. When asked for an opinion, I said that if I were going to drive from San Francisco to New York on a very important journey, I would not select the finest automobile built in 1919 or use as a guide the best road map of that year. Further, that Freud himself, with his marvelous and ever-searching mind, would certainly have moved far beyond what he was doing seventy-five years ago. In addition, he never did this kind of analysis but was very far from the "blank screen" or "mirror analyst." He was active and interactive, and his analyses were far, far shorter.

The world, as William James described in his Hibbert Lectures in Oxford in 1908, is "unfenced, uncultivated, untidy and unpredictable" (p. 19). In spite of all our attempts to make it fenced, cultivated, tidy, and predictable (attempts like the modern system of clarifying our patients, the *DSM* series), our patients still fit the James picture. If we wish to help them, we had better learn to put up with this truth.

James regarded attempts to make exact measurements of human consciousness as "a patent whimsey of that dear old man" [William Fechner] and refused to put any such attempts in his *Principles of Psychology* (Perry 1935, p. 588).

And the problem has other serious implications. It is an old problem but one of which we rarely speak. Why do so many of our best, and best trained and analyzed, suffer psychological breakdowns of one sort or another? Why in recent years have the ex-heads of such organizations as the American Psychiatric Association and the Holistic Medical Association lost their licenses for improper relations with patients? Don't we all know that what has surfaced into public knowledge is only a small percentage of what might? To keep this in perspective, however, we also know that many of the best trained of gurus, often people who have spent years in extensive meditation and study, also have an unusually high frequency of breakdown. The long-trained and experienced head of a major Eastern spiritual development organization, knowing he had AIDS, had unprotected intercourse with a large number of his devotees and said in explanation that he believed that his karma would protect them. From the one who owned literally dozens of Rolls Royces to the ones who insist on celibacy among their devotees and then are revealed as using some of these as sexual objects themselves, the litany is long and sorrowful.

(Then there are the gurus who explain that sex is a way for the teacher to pass on wisdom to the student—in short, that it is a teaching device. Curiously, in most cases it is a cross-sex device; students of the opposite sex from the guru benefit by it; those of the same sex do not need it. Whether or not the determination of whether a particular student will benefit by this teaching method is related to his or her sexual attractiveness is a matter for future studies, but I would be willing to lay bets on the outcome of that research.)

It is not a new problem. Freud wrote in 1932:

> To me it appears to be the greatest disappointment in analysis that it does not effect a greater change in the analysts themselves. No one has yet made a subject of study the means by which analysts succeed in evading the influence of analysis on their own persons. [pp. 6–7]

We mostly refrain from commenting, even to ourselves, on the obvious fact that if we look around us at those who have had long and arduous training and self-study and are generally now in the position of either being full-time therapists or else spending some time training and analyzing the next generation, we find a group whose personal lives often leave a lot to be desired and some of whom are frankly pretty peculiar and often hard to get along with. The infighting and prestige hunting among the leaders in psychological, psychiatric, and psychoanalytic societies reinforces this point.

Nor do we do much better when we look at the most admired saints of our present and past times. Gandhi was frequently unjust, tyrannical, and authoritarian to the members of his own family. Schweitzer's bringing

a sick wife in her later years to possibly the worst and
most debilitating climate on earth reveals a problem
of some magnitude. Tolstoy's family life as revealed
by his wife's speech at his funeral left a good deal to be
desired. Evelyn Underhill, the brilliant encyclopedist
of mysticism, writing of the religious saints points
out that before they were saints they were men and that
they frequently remained narrow in outlook, intensely
prejudiced, harsh, cruel, and monomaniacal, to say the
least.

The problem is widespread. Why does our best and
most intensive training not provide a way of growth and
becoming to the full-time practitioners, to, as Freud
said, "the analysts themselves," that would bring them
to a level of being and functioning where we would not
see as much sick behavior as we do? What is wrong with
our methods of gardening human beings that it does
not do more for the gardeners?

Is it perhaps that there is one basic fallacy that runs
through all our approaches? And, if so, what might that
fallacy be?

The poet Sara Teasdale wrote:

> I made you many and many a song
> But none told all you are—
> It was as though a net of words
> Were flung to catch a star.
>
> It was as though I curved my hand
> And dipped sea water eagerly,
> Only to find it lost the blue
> Dark splendor of the sea.

If the poet, with the poet's global technique, cannot find
one image that covers all that is important about a
human being, how can the scientist with the analytic

techniques of science hope to? Or, for that matter, the mystic with the techniques of mysticism?

In my undergraduate days I had a marvelous teacher of psychology, Dick Henneman. A required course was a year-long, five-hour-a-week course in the history and systems of psychology. The first session Henneman began with a psychoanalytic viewpoint. For six weeks he taught this viewpoint with fire and zeal, and at the end of that time, we were all convinced that this system was the correct and only one to use if we wished to understand human beings and their inner and outer lives. Then suddenly one session he switched to a behavioristic viewpoint and taught this with the same fire, zeal, and scorn of other viewpoints. Later he switched again to a personalistic viewpoint and later to a Gestalt approach, and then to others. At the end of the course we all knew that each of these theoretical approaches had validity but that none owned exclusive rights to the territory, that all systems are incomplete—all systems of explanation of a human being limp.

Later in my training this was reinforced by a dedicated training analyst, Joseph Michaels, who was my chief. He taught us that there are analytic patients in certain situations who should be approached with an analytic theory and viewpoint; that there are Jungian, Adlerian, Existentialist, and GOK (God Only Knows) patients; and that there is no one right way to view all and treat all our patients but a best way for this person at this time.

All the major systems cover some of the territory and leave some of it out. They all limp. However, it is the dedicated practitioners who believe most strongly in the system, who most deeply believe that their system, whichever it is, applies to the total human being *including themselves* and the total human condition *includ-*

ing their own. They believe deeply in a model of the human being that leaves something out of what it means to be human. Each model or system, if followed this completely, leaves the person with, we might say, a vitamin deficiency of the organism or, if you wish, of the mind or the soul. Applying this system to themselves as well as others, they leave out and reject a basic part of themselves. There is bound to be, as we all know well from our training, a heavy price to pay for this. Is it possible that it is this pressure that accounts for the disturbing behavior we see in so many of our best-trained human gardeners?

I am reminded here of the advice of Rabelais that if you wish to live in peace, joy, and health and to be merry, "never trust men that always peep out through a little hole." We have been warned about this and the problem pointed up time and again. In his 1895 presidential address to the American Psychological Association, J. McKeen Cattell (1978) said:

> We are past the time for simple explanations and systems, *for metaphysics which explain everything in one way*. The physiologist Ludwig in the 1880s wrote a classic textbook *Physiology* which explained everything on one basis—mechanism. Later he was asked why he did not prepare a new edition of it. He said, *"Such a work must be written by a young man; an older man is too aware of his ignorance*. [italics added: p. 53]

I have written elsewhere (LeShan 1990) of the problem we in the social sciences have in our tendency to make a single model of what a human being is and then to explain all aspects of humanity on the basis of that single model. Each time a new model is invented or an old one again becomes chic we generally give in to the temptation to use it as a total explanatory system. The reflex, the birth order, the-brain-as-computer, the-mind-as-hydraulic-pump, the drive to self-realization, the fixation at a particular stage of development, karma, the-human-as-white-rat, the mind as a servomechanism, the switchboard analogy—all have seemed from time to time and school to school to be a useful way of understanding everything about human consciousness and behavior. And each time we do this—explain everything about a human being on the basis of one model —we do violence to the state of being human and to the person we are describing. I can discuss Oedipus, Sigmund Freud, B. F. Skinner, Richard the Lionhearted, Robert E. Lee, Winston Churchill, Baron Richtoven, or you in any of these terms. However, when I am finished I have a flat, two-dimensional picture. The person is lost. Further, if I deeply believe in the explanatory system, *as do most thoroughly trained leaders in each, and apply it to myself,* I do violence to myself. I, at the least, leave out some part of myself and deny its validity. Laying such violent hands on the self puts a heavy pressure on our stability.

Could this be the common factor running through our observations that the best trained of our psychoanalysts and mystics often live at a level so far below what we all know is the human potential?

It is so hard for us to keep open to new experience and new interpretations. It is hard for us to look for the best metaphor for *this* patient at *this* time in his or her life and not ruthlessly apply our favorite metaphor of the moment or the metaphor used by the school that trained us. It is even harder to keep in mind that all our knowledge and all our metaphors are tentative and that the next patient who comes into our office may be the one to force us into a major revision of our ideas if we can only observe without having made up our minds in advance as to what frame of reference we are going to use no matter what the patient is, says, and does. How much more we might have learned by now if we could only do this occasionally! What new concepts we might have!

> Like the earth of a hundred years ago, our mind still has its darkest Africas, its unmapped Borneos and Amazonian basins. In relation to the fauna of these regions we are not yet zoologists, we are mere naturalists and collectors of specimens. . . . Like the giraffe and the duckbilled platypus, the creatures inhabiting these remote regions of the mind are exceedingly improbable. [Huxley 1963, p. 85]

It is not only that we hold back our knowledge from advancing by imprinting our expectations on our observations and so block our learning of anything new. It is also that we often harm our patients by insisting that they are what we expect rather than what they are. I recall one disturbing experience toward the end of 1945 that was half comic and nearly half tragic resulting from this tendency.

When the German prisoner of war camps were liberated by the advancing Allied forces in World War II, the first thing done was to set up a medical evaluation system so that each ex-prisoner could get whatever medical treatment he needed after his harsh imprisonment. One ex-prisoner refused to have anything to do with this, claiming he had no time for it, that he must immediately speak to an intelligence officer. An intelligence officer was sent for and a major appeared. The prisoner refused to talk with him, claiming that he had personal instructions from President Roosevelt, delivered in the Oval Office, not to talk to anyone but an intelligence officer at or above the rank of full colonel.

Since this was clearly so typical of many of the delu-
sions developed in POW camps, he was asked to wait
for a few minutes "in there." The "in there," of course,
was a locked psychiatric ward. He made two attempts
to break out, in one of them putting two wardmen in
the hospital with severe fractures. He was flown back
to the United States in restraints and wound up in Newton D. Baker Army hospital in West Virginia where I
was stationed. For reasons that now escape me, the hospital was, at that time, using electroshock for treating
paranoid schizophrenia, which was all over his chart
and was the admitting diagnosis. While he was being
worked up for the shock treatment, the Red Cross had
notified his wife that he was in the hospital. She appeared, was allowed to see him, stayed fifteen minutes,
and left. Two hours later the chief of the hospital got a
call from the Pentagon (eighty miles away) with the
furious order to fly Captain "Smith" to Washington
immediately. Twenty minutes later a staff car left the
hospital for the local airfield with Captain Smith in the
back and the chief of the hospital on one side of him
and the chief of psychiatry on the other, making the best
nice-nice they could.

From the Inspector-General's men, who were all
over the hospital and looking over all our shoulders for
the next few months, we learned what had happened.
In one of the most secret projects of the war, a small
group of specialists were trained and dropped into
Germany by parachute some months before Germany
surrendered. Their mission was to track the big Nazis
as they went into hiding and make it possible for us to
capture and try them. The mission had to be kept secret because if the Germans found out about it, the
Gestapo would have made a major effort to kill the

agents who could be exposed by their tracking activities. The evening before the group was flown to England, Roosevelt had them brought to the Oval Office and warned them that the American Intelligence Service was compromised and that they were *on no account* to talk about their work to anyone except an American intelligence officer at or above the rank of full colonel. This particular man had been captured, passed himself off as a commando, had been sent to the POW camp, and was awaiting execution there when the camp was liberated.

It was a lesson that taught us all caution. I remember that several months later a soldier was brought into the hospital because he had carved crosses on his paratroop boots and claimed to be Jesus Christ returned to earth to bring peace. We, on the staff, felt very unsure as to how to proceed and, after much hesitation, finally discharged him from the Army and sent him to a veterans' hospital. We felt ashamed of our hesitation and lack of confidence as to what to do. Today, nearly half a century later and with a great deal more experience under my belt, I would be even more hesitant and unsure.

A rather similar event had occurred a number of years earlier. During my senior year at college, I worked part-time in running the hydrotherapy room at Eastern State Asylum (sic!) in Williamsburg, Virginia. In the predominantly rural catchment area of the hospital was a family consisting of several brothers and the wives and children of two of them. The whole family was generally regarded as being rather low-grade—not exactly at Jukes and Kallikaks level, but not too high above it, either. The youngest brother was what we would call today "intellectually challenged" but what we then diagnosed as medium- to high-grade moron level. He made his living by hiring himself out as an assistant ditch digger, latrine cleaner, and so forth.

One day he came to the police station claiming that his brothers were trying to kill him by "dropping the house on me." He could not seem to give any further details but was very agitated and half threatening and half fearful. The police brought him to the hospital where he was admitted after questioning the other brothers who claimed he had "been getting crazier and crazier for days now," and he was placed on a closed ward where he remained for several years.

At that time one of the other brothers was in a truck accident and made a deathbed confession that the story had indeed been true. Houses in that area were generally built on pillars of flat rocks, piled one on the other to a height of about three feet. This was to provide an air space and to keep the floor dry in heavy rains. For reasons that remained unclear after the confession, they decided to kill the youngest brother. This seemed to be motivated by quarrels, by the need for more space as new children were produced, and by other unspecified causes. They tried to murder him by playing ball in front of the house, by throwing it past him and under the house, and then when he went into the underfloor part to get it, by hitting two of the pillars with sledgehammers so as to drop the house on him and then be able to claim it had been an accident. After several years in a back ward, however, with the primitive treatment available at that time and place, I have heard (I had left the area by then) that he was too deteriorated to release.

I believe that every experienced psychotherapist has, if he or she will recall, been involved in incidents of the sort illustrated by these two stories. We all need to keep in mind, in all our patient evaluations, "I might be completely wrong!"

The real moral of these incidents, and the many similar, if perhaps less dramatic ones that all experienced therapists can remember, is that we must be careful not to confuse our theories about the human mind with reality. They are often useful and fruitful metaphors, but they are not the reality of "what really happened." They are our interpretation of events. René Magritte has a famous painting of a tobacco pipe. It is a very realistic painting. Under it is written *"Ceci n'est pas un pipe"*—this is not a pipe. It is not; it is the picture of a pipe.

Not only must we be careful not to confuse our interpretations with reality, we must be careful not to confuse them with the patient's experience. No matter how close, how caring, how empathic, how well trained we are, we are still at a distance. Goethe put it, "Gray are all your theories, but green the growing tree of life."

————◆·————

Many years ago a patient and I were working together. I made a comment about something or other, and she replied, "Larry, I can't stand it any longer. In some areas you are too ignorant to be allowed to live! I have been coming to you for a year now. It is time you came to me. The Hapsburg Art Collection is in town. You are going to spend two afternoons with me learning how to look at a painting!"

The next week I did spend two afternoons in the museum with her. Jane taught me that you must first look at a picture on *its* terms before you bring out your own. Before you comment to yourself about it, you look at it and let it speak to you. Then you react to what is there instead of what you expected or wanted to be in the painting.

It was an invaluable lesson. It applies very strongly to our work as psychotherapists. One of our hardest tasks is to apply this to our patients. Before you react, plan, interpret (even to yourself), to let the patient speak on his own terms. What is *his* world? All that you know in advance is that it will be different than yours.

Compare in your mind the world lived in by the club-footed physician–protaganist of *Of Human Bondage*, Philip Carey, and that of the prostitute Sadie Thompson, the main figure in another work of Somerset Maugham, *Rain*. Their worlds, how they see themselves and reality, are very different. An interpretation that makes sense in one is wrong or irrelevant in the other. Your next two patients' worlds are just as different.

When we do let patients speak to us on their own terms before we interpret and react and interpret, we avoid many mistakes and confusions. One woman told me that when she was 8 or 9, her school gave psychological tests to the students. One question on one of the tests was "You are all alone, walking on a bridge over a river. How do you feel? What would you do?" She had answered it by saying that she would jump off. The psychologist was very upset about this and called her mother to come to the school. When the mother arrived, she was shown this response and was told that her daughter was clearly suicidal and needed immediate help if not hospitalization. The mother laughed and told the psychologist that her daughter was a superb swimmer and was just now getting lessons in diving, which she loved, and that her greatest pleasure was to dive into water from the highest platforms she could find.

Another patient was, at 3 or 4, given a test in which she was told to draw a line between pictures of a chair and a table. To the psychologist's surprise she drew a flower. Later she told her mother about this. She said that she had been told to draw a lion between the two pictures. "But I don't know how to draw a lion so I drew a daisy." When her mother said that she was probably told to draw a line, the child replied, "Oh, no, it couldn't have been that. That would have been too easy!" I leave it to you, however, to imagine what the typical psychologist's reaction would have been to the drawing.

Or imagine the scoring and interpretation to another response of the same child. Asked to complete the series "The fox ate the two little rabbits. The fox ate the three little rabbits. The fox ate the four little rabbits. The fox ate the [dash] little rabbits," the child replied, "Poor." No computer-friendly scoring system—and, unfortunately, very few psychologists—would give this response the high score for compassion and relatedness-to-the-world (and other categories that are important for the future of our species and for understanding this child) that it deserves.

The concept of the IQ was first invented by the psychologist William Stern when he was, in his words, "a very young man." Stern's deepest wish in his later years was to introduce the concept of the Person and Personalistic Psychology in America in order "to counteract the pernicious effect of my earlier invention, the IQ."

The concept of the IQ was more technically developed in the early twentieth century by Alfred Binet and Theodore Simon. Here was the first time we had techniques to *define numerically* a meaningful part of human personality; we felt very scientific. The Binet-Simon Intelligence test was widely diffused and used and variations of all kinds were made of it.

The IQ field today is in such a mess that in 1984 the police in New York came up with a rather original solution to the problems it raised. African-American and Hispanic policemen had claimed that the intelligence tests used for sergeants ratings were unfair to them and demanded a new one. They were given permission to commission a new test, and they selected a company to design one for them. They then examined and approved the result. However, the new test also passed a higher percentage of Caucasian than African-American and Hispanic applicants. After the test had been given, they and the organization that had selected the company doing the design reported that the test was "fair" but that the *results* were discriminating and that the test should be scrapped!

In the early 1970s, Theodore Simon (to the great surprise of most psychologists, who had assumed that he was long dead) wrote a letter to the major psychology journal, *The American Psychologist*. He deplored the widespread use of, and the importance given to, what he described as a minor and unimportant tool that he and Binet had devised to help teachers check some of their impressions of students in certain types of difficulty. It should not, wrote the pioneer, be used for anything else.

Sixty years of intelligence testing of children have taught us very little, if anything, about children that we did not already know. Intelligence testing has, however, made very real contributions to statistical theory that are not applicable to any specific child. It has also damaged a great many children who believed in the validity of the concept or whose parents or teachers did.

So far as I know, the only truly intelligent use made of the concept was in the United States Army in World War II. They used a very good group intelligence test, the Army General Classification Test (AGCT), to indicate that *this* soldier, at *this* time of his life, in the presence of sufficient motivation, leadership, and various personality and experience categories, could successfully pass through certain Army schools. The qualifiers were always very clear. If a concept is so basically flawed that just about the only organization using it intelligently is the Army, everyone else had better be pretty careful with it.

There is no question but that the IQ tests and testers have flunked their "examinations." The purpose of their work was to show that they could predict behavior. They could not. Further, when examined as a group, the test designers violently disagreed on what they were testing. As Seymour Sarason (1981) has pointed out, "The concept of intelligence is a social invention, inevitably reflecting social time and place, not a 'thing' in an individual" (p. 111). A person's pancreas or brain may have a definite size—not his or her intelligence.

Further, as the IQ became so popular and so widely accepted, it often had unlooked-for effects on public policy. When H. H. Goddard (of Jukes and Kallikaks fame) tested immigrants at Ellis Island with the Binet-Simon Intelligence Test, he found that 83 percent of Jews, 80 percent of Hungarians, 79 percent of Italians, and 87 percent of Russians were feebleminded. These results had a strong effect on the immigration policies of the United States.

When Frederic Wyatt was teaching us about testing in the Veterans Administration in the late 1940s, he once showed us a curious response to the "ball-in-the-field" test. In this test, a circle drawn on a sheet of paper is shown to the person being tested. He is told that this is a field in which a ball has been lost. He is given a pencil and told to draw the path he would take in searching for the ball. Any organized and coherent response is scored as correct. The man, after some thought, drew

several crosses in the circle and then traced a path going from one cross to the next and circling each one
before going onto the next. We all agreed that this was
to be scored as a failure. Then Wyatt told us that he
had questioned the man about it and found out that
he came from an area in the southern mountains
where there were no open fields. He had played ball
as a child in the best places available. These were small
pastures with trees growing here and there in them.
From his experience, he had drawn in the trees (the
crosses) and knew that the best place to look for a lost
ball was around the roots of the trees. He had given a
correct and valid response to the test, but his experience was so different than ours that we scored it in-
correctly.

In the same period, a Rorschach was given by one
of the students to a Veteran's Administration patient.
The responses were so unusual that we spent hours trying to interpret them. There was clearly "flattening of
the ego," "perceptual blocking," and a variety of other
pathologies present. After we agreed that (in spite of a
lack of clinical symptoms) we were dealing with a rare
and classic case of early "simple schizophrenia," we
showed the protocols to Wyatt. He looked at them for
a few minutes, smiled, and said, "The real diagnosis is
'color-blind.'" He was right. The patient lived in a color-
less world, far different than ours.

In World War II in an Army General Hospital, the
chief of psychiatry, Joseph Michaels, was trying to teach
us how to look at our patients as individuals and not to
jump to conclusions as to diagnoses. In a staff conference, he asked us what we would think of a patient who
saw things no one else did. We all agreed that this was
a definitive sign of psychosis. Then Michaels brought
into the room a soldier who worked as a cook in the

hospital. After introducing him to the group, Michaels asked, "Have you ever seen something no one else did?" The soldier replied, "Once I was sitting on the porch and I said to my mammy, 'What is that man doing by the brook?'" and she said, 'Don't pay no attention to him, son, he's just a ghost.'"

Michaels then sent the soldier on his way and told us that this man was a fully functioning, sane person with no signs of psychosis. He came from the bayou country in Louisiana, and in his particular subculture, it was common to see ghosts that often only one person could see at a time. What would be psychotic in our world was normal and sane in his.

———◆———

That we *must* regard each person as a unique individual and that classifications into groups and statistical ratings tend to hide (at least) as much as they reveal, is shown by the constant problems we have with mental health scales and with "observer ratings." Both those on the "healthy" end of these classification systems and those on the "sick" end are the most likely to be disturbed. Soldiers who looked the most healthy on mental health scales were as likely to break down as those on the other extreme, and both were more likely to break down than those in the middle ranges (Rose 1956). Cancer patients who self-reported high levels of mental health tended statistically to die sooner then those who reported greater distress (Derogatis et al. 1979).

In the words of Rabbi Nachman, "God never does the same thing twice." The geneticist Dobzhansky wrote in 1960 that human beings have, in principle, 10^{1000} (10 to the 1,000th power) different gene possibilities present. This is a number larger than the total number of atoms in the universe. Only a small number of these possibilities can ever be realized, but, he concludes, each individual is the carrier of a completely unique genotype (de Vries 1994).

This is reminiscent of the statement Trigant Burrow used to make—that "normality" is an illness because it does violence to the uniqueness of the person and his or her one-of-a kind path.

In remaining constantly aware of the differences between each of our patients, it is essential that we remember that it is not only in ways of being, relating, creating, in the best form of exercise, nutrition, meditation, and so forth, that differ for this unique, one-of-a-kind person in front of us. They also differ in what is meaningful to them. No person can remain vital, enthusiastic, *alive*, without a goal that means something to them. "Life," wrote Hegel, "has no value unless it holds something of value in front of it." What is "worthwhile" to *this* person? This is not something that the person can be convinced of no matter how strongly the therapist believes in it. It is something that grows organically out of the person's whole existence. The therapist can help remove the blocks that keep the person from being aware of what is meaningful for him: the therapist cannot tell the patient what is the right thing to find meaningful. The patient must discover it himself when the special problems that have prevented him from doing this are solved.

The therapeutic situation is similar to that of the patient who comes to us because he cannot love. We are clear that we cannot tell him whom to fall in love with or when. What we can do is help him grow past the factors that have prevented him from loving and then wait until he, at his own pace and of his own choice, falls in love. Similarly in finding a reason for his existence, argument and precept are worse than useless. It must come from within or not at all.

We recognize the importance of the people we work with being able to learn to love. Less often are we aware of the equal if not greater importance of their finding a reason for their existence. Ernest Becker (1969) put it:

> If I were asked for the single most striking insight into human nature and the human condition, it would be this: that no person is strong enough to support the meaning of his life unaided by something outside him. [p. 130]

This is a partial truth. It would be more valid to say that no person can keep his existence vital and alive without a goal that means something to him. There must be a reason for existence, a *raison d'être*. Additionally, we have found that its absence tends to lead the immune system to function at a lower level and the person is in increased danger of physically breaking down.

When the individual finds a *raison d'être* that involves him in a goal, the immune system begins to function more strongly. It is no accident that when a country becomes emotionally involved in a war (as England, 1914–1918 or 1939–1945), the cancer mortality rate drops sharply and stays down as long as the war continues. Or that it rises sharply in the five years after the age of forced retirement from work, whether that age be 55, 60, 65, or 70. Our total organismic integration and resilience lowers unless there is a meaning to our life.

This is critical for our work as psychotherapists and our individual existence as human beings. We are not seeking simply to reduce tensions but to change them.

Our goal—in work and in life—is growth and action, finding peace through the use of our energy in the ways syntonic, natural to us as individuals—not in finding pleasant graves while we are still breathing. In Viktor Frankl's words:

> Mental health is based on a certain degree of tension, the tension between what one has already achieved and what one still ought to accomplish, or the gap between what one is and what one should accomplish. [quoted in Willis 1994, p. 202]

One way of approaching this is to try to be aware, before a person comes into the office, that people come to us with their pain, their fears, their hopes, their joys. They bring these to the office and when they do, we suddenly are on holy ground. We understand the meaning of the last lines of Yeats's (1899) poem "He Wishes for the Cloths of Heaven":

> I have spread my dreams under your feet;
> Tread softly because you tread on my dreams.

We must tread softly because we are dealing with the sacred. Those of us who have kept on growing and try to be honest with ourselves look backward now and then with shame and sadness for the times when someone has brought their dreams to us and we, with the best intentions, have—since we were committed to a particular metaphor or method that did not fit this individual—walked on them with hobnailed boots.

> These clumsy feet, still in the mire
> Go crushing blossoms without end.
> These hard, well-meaning hands we thrust
> Among the heartstrings of a friend.

The ill-timed truth we might have kept
Who knows how deep it pierced and stung?
The word we had not sense to say,
Who knows how grandly it had rung?
[Edward Rowland Sill, "The Fool's Prayer,"
quoted in McGraw 1934, p. 432]

Part of the reason we must treat each patient as an individual is simple—so simple that we frequently forget it. Patients come to us to learn to relate better—to themselves and to others. If we are to teach them this, or even help them learn it, we must relate well to them. And relating well to a person means relating to *this* person, to treat them as a unique individual.

If we respond in a mechanical, one-size-fits-all manner, we may be able to use our techniques and our knowledge to help them solve a particular problem and pain. This is not a small gift and one not to be dismissed lightly. As long as we are using the medical model that health is the absence of disabling and/or painful symptoms, it is enough for us to cure. However, if we wish to live up to the best of our tradition and help our patients learn to grow and to heal themselves, learn to cure new problems as they arise, we need to be nonmechanical and to treat our patients as if each was a unique individual and this is to be respected.

————•————

In 1959, the New York University Institute of Philosophy held an extensive symposium on the similarities and differences between human beings and machines. Does the human mind operate according to computer principles? Can machines think? Are the two fundamentally different? These were the basic questions studied. Many of the leading figures in philosophy, psychology, brain function, and computer design attended and spoke.

The discussion covered the field and seemed to be reaching no agreement. Then Paul Weiss pointed out a fundamental difference. After pointing out that machines, at least in principle, could be developed that would do the things human beings do, he said that the crucial difference was in our ability to love.

> We will, in short, divide beings, all of whom behave in the same way, into two classes, calling "men" those which are in principle within our powers to love, and calling "machines" those which we cannot possibly love. . . .
>
> Both what cannot be loved by one who can love, and what cannot love what can be loved, are less than human, no matter how much they look like and behave like men. Machines fail on both counts. They are not on a footing with me. . . . The conclusion is not surprising, for we all know that a machine is an artifact whose parts are united so as to enable them to act together, whereas a man is a unity in which the whole governs the behavior of the parts. Only such a unity has a self, with feelings, mind, will, and the rest. [Hook 1966, p. 179]

When we cannot love a patient with whom we are working, this is a sign that we are seeing him as a collection of parts whose interactions need to be rearranged before they can function according to our standards. And we are teaching the patient to view and treat himself as a machine to be fixed, not as a person to be loved.

———— • ◆ • ————

There is, as Thomas Merton (1957) has pointed out, a real distinction between love and friendship. We can love our patients and wish and work wholeheartedly for the best for them. "To love another is to wish what is really good for him. Such love must be based on truth and on an accurate understanding of what and who this person is. . . . Love not only prefers the good of the other person to our own, but it does not even compare the two." Friendship, however, is based on having a great deal in common with another person. This is rare, and intimate friendship is correspondingly rare.

> We can be, in some sense, friends to all men because there is no man on earth with whom we do not have something in common. But it would be false to treat too many men as intimate friends. It is not possible to be intimate with more than very few, because there are only very few in the world with whom we have practically everything in common. [Merton 1957, p. 32]

It should not be necessary here to add the following, but such is the state of our art that it is. Love for the patient does not include sexual relations. When this happens, it is exploitative of the patient no matter how good the rationalizations of the therapist. A well-known California psychiatrist once told me that he had found that with certain patients it was necessary to have one night together in bed "in order to close up the transference." However, he was very ethical about this, he told me, as he waited for a period of at least two months after the therapy had finished. I asked him if there was a stronger need for this in his younger and more attractive patients than there was in the older or the less attractive ones. He thought seriously about this for a few minutes and then said, with some surprise, that, indeed, on the basis of his experience, my suggestion was valid and he wondered why this was so. I suggested he think about it, and he said he would!

Psychotherapy might well be defined as the second best way to get to know and understand another human being. (The first way, of course, is to fall in love with him or her.) However, this is not quite true. In order to be effective, therapy must have the characteristic of the therapist unequivocably wanting the best for the patient whatever this is, even if it is a goal or a way of life far from what would be of value to the therapist for her own life. To want the best for another person and to care deeply about this is as good a definition of love as you are likely to find anywhere.

Thus, for the therapy to be effective and heal, the therapist must love the patient. Without this, it is all mechanics and we may cure, but we cannot heal.

In the beginning years of psychotherapy, during the first half or three-quarters of the century, it was generally believed that the technical ability of the therapist was the major factor in determining the success of the treatment (assuming that the patient was treatable at all). The general idea was that the patient should seek the most technically skilled and the most qualified therapist.

In the past quarter-century or so, we have begun to realize that that technical ability in a particular method or school of psychotherapy was absolutely necessary, but far from sufficient. First, that there is no one method of therapy right for all patients or patient–therapist pairs. Second, that technical ability apart from maturity and continued growth on the part of the therapist often meant little more than that the therapist had an organized warehouse of tricks and gimmicks that sometimes helped cure the patient of specific problems.

The belief that most of us hold, that if we apply correctly the method that our mentors taught us we would cure all those who were curable, has been wide-spread in our field since the middle years of Freud's research. It came to us, via him, from a general belief in the late-eighteenth and early-nineteenth centuries that all nature could be dealt with by a certain kind of process called an algorithm. In this process, all steps are followed each time, all are in order. If followed correctly each of the small steps invariably leads to the correct result. An example we are all familiar with is long division. In this no great decisions have to be made —all the steps are small and follow inexorably from each other. If you do them in the correct order, you automatically arrive at the right answer.

It was believed at that time that the whole universe was determined and could be dealt with by the correct algorithm. The formal process of psychoanalysis was seen as such a process. Today, through hard experience (generally harder for our patients than for ourselves!), we have learned better. There are no algorithms in psychotherapy whether you are a Freudian, a Jungian, a Behavior Modification therapist (a contradiction in terms if I ever heard one!), an Existentialist, a Humanistic or Eclectic Therapist, or any other subspecies of our confused and hopeful profession. There are no algorithms, there is only the possibility of growth, becoming, and a shared adventure.

Today we advise prospective patients to shop for a therapist with the expenditure of at least as much time and energy as in deciding on which make of new car they would buy. Assuming technical proficiency on the basis of membership in relevant professional organizations (and asking the therapist about background, training, and the amount of therapy he or she has had and whether or not they have, at present, someone they consult with—a control, they should, after the first session, find a quiet spot and seriously ask themselves some specific questions.

1. Does this person seem to know what he or she is doing? Granted no one knows much about anyone else until after ten or fifteen sessions (at the least), does this person seem to be "with it"? To have a sense of what wave length I am on?
2. Do I *like* this person? Is this someone who, as I get to know him or her better, I will find it easier to talk to about very personal things? If you did not meet a person in the first session but just a mask and a set of formal questions and/or responses, get out. Psychotherapy is not a human–computer interaction.
3. Did this therapist seem to be trying to meet and relate to me *as an individual* and *unique person,* or do I have the sense I was put into a classification system and responded to as a member of a class? Put differently, did the therapist seem to be saying, "Together let's find *your* dreams and how to fulfill them. We will celebrate where you are and find how *you* can thrive the best in your way."? Or did the therapist seem to have a blueprint of what was wrong with you and what "curing" you would mean?

Unless the answers to these three questions come out right, we now tell prospective patients "shop further." Keep trying out possible therapists until the answers are correct—until the answers say that this can be a relationship in which *your* individuality and specialness are recognized and valued. In which you can love and be loved. One that can provide an environment in which *you* can do the hardest thing in the world—become more yourself.

"Psychotherapy," wrote James Bugental in 1965, "is not a healing process. It is a philosophic venture. It is daring to confront self-and-world" (p. 42).

If you have two patients who are on the same adventure, making the same "philosophic venture" into the unknown, and needing the same kind of help, it means you do not know very much about one or both of them.

———•◆•———

3

THE GOALS
AND METHODS
OF PSYCHOTHERAPY

The fact that we model for our patients by the lives we lead clearly does not mean that we must spend time talking about our own lives and our own development. What we are and how we lead our lives is largely transmitted by the unconscious to unconscious communication that takes place in a real therapeutic encounter. Unless we are working at our own growth and becoming, our encouragement to the patient to work at his is somehow flat and unconvincing. Our task is harder and takes much longer—if it succeeds at all. However, there is a clear line between modeling and using the patient as a paying audience while we talk about our own life.

It should not be necessary to discuss this except for the fact that many therapists spend much time in discussing their own exploits in life. They have swung to the opposite extreme of the older view that we *never* reveal anything personal about ourselves so that we can remain the blank screen on which the patient can project his transference needs. Of the two extremes, it is very probable that the older one of the therapist's invisibility does far less damage to the process than its opposite.

One experienced and *formally* well-trained therapist I knew was fascinated by musical theater. She got a tremendous amount of zest and enjoyment out of this way of creative expression and participated in shows and exhibitions all over the country. With patients she frequently discussed this and showed them her costumes and videos of her performances.

She had one patient whom she had helped very much with a real crisis. This woman, who had left therapy about two years before, called her and asked for a session. The therapist had only forty-five minutes available and made the appointment. During the two-year interval the patient's father had died (a matter of great anguish to her), she had achieved a lifelong ambition and changed careers with much anxiety, and she had taken the greatest risk of her life by moving to a completely different kind of life than she had ever lived before. One would think that there was plenty of material for a forty-five minute session. However, when the patient returned home, she told her husband a very large number of details as to where the therapist had been acting and singing in the interval, the parts she had had, her success in Canada and what she had worn there, and so forth. The patient, of course, never had had a chance to discuss what was very much on her mind, nor did she ever return to the therapist.

One kind of situation in which I have frequently seen this type of acting-out is when therapists are working with patients with catastrophic disease. Often the patient is in the sick mode and is oriented to discussing his life, the stresses in it, and what to do in order to recover. The therapist, however, with a large amount of anxiety over the subject of death, keeps trying to prepare the patient for dying as if the patient were in the dying mode. The therapist is trying to solve his own existential problems in the wrong way at the wrong time and at the expense of the patient.

The modeling versus acting-out problem is one of the reasons that supervision is needed for the whole of our professional lives. Hopefully, if the therapist who enjoyed musical theater so much had been in supervision, her acting-out would have been picked up and handled and her patients spared a good deal of unnecessary pain.

A therapist who is not in supervision should be regarded either with suspicion or awe. He or she is making a statement that they have learned all that is needed for one of the most complex problems in existence—helping others to be as fully human as possible and to survive and exult in being in the human condition. If they have arrived at this august state (I, personally, have never met anyone who has), they deserve our awe; otherwise, our suspicion.

Further, the therapist is saying that his knowledge of what it means to be human is so extensive that it includes the patient and the patient's fears, hopes and joys, and that there is nothing in him which would block his understanding of the myriad facets of humanity. This is a tall claim, to put it mildly. We never get over the need for this, no matter our experience and training, no matter how far along our own path we have come.

I remember clearly that once, when Marthe Gassmann was my supervisor, she asked me about a par-

ticular patient—"Bobbie." I replied that Bobbie was fine
but that I had two real problems with patients coming
in that afternoon and needed to talk about them. She
answered, "But first tell me about Bobbie. You haven't
mentioned her for some time." I answered that Bobbie
was, as I had said, fine, and she replied, "Tell me about
Bobbie," and I burst into completely unexpected tears.
Bobbie, with whom I had worked for two years, was
dying and I had been unable to face it. Instead, to spare
myself the pain of her coming death, I had withdrawn
emotionally from her and thereby fulfilled her worst
fantasy. "If I let someone see me as I really am, then if
I ever need them, they will leave me." I had kept seeing
Bobbie at the usual intervals and in the usual ways, but
without any emotional involvement. Literally a ghost
or empty hulk came into her room. After Gassmann
made me see, explore, and feel what was going on, I was
able to return to her emotionally and stay there until
she died.

With another patient who had died, Gassmann and
I were going over the transcripts and saw that at least a
dozen times in the four months before his death, he had
tried to bring up a particular subject and each time I
had blocked him off from discussing it. He had tried
over and over again to talk about his internationally
famous and successful-in-everything brother and their
feelings for each other. The following sessions between
Gassmann and myself explored my feelings for *my*
golden-haired and successful brother who had been the
darling of the family and eclipsed me in every way. I
do not believe that I will block in that area again, but I
also know that there are other, unsuspected areas in
which I will, and unless someone else (with different
areas of blockage!) is looking over my shoulder, I will
be doing a disservice, at the least, to my patients.

When selecting a therapist or a control supervisor, it is perfectly legitimate to ask, "Do you have a control therapist [a supervisor]?" If the answer is no, I *strongly* advise looking further. (It is also advisable to ask, "How much intensive personal therapy have you had?" Unless the answer is [at least] a couple of years, go to the nearest exit at once.)

————•◆•————

One reason why modeling is so central is that we are hoping to help the patient change his attitudes toward himself and his feelings and experiences. In contrast to facts, attitudes (in the words of one psychoanalyst) cannot be taught—they must be caught.

It is important for the therapist to be clear that the facts, including the facts of our internal life, are less important than our attitudes toward them. How we feel about our experiences and our feelings is more important in determining how we behave and are than these experiences and feelings themselves. Victor Frankl used to try to illustrate this point in his lectures by telling the story of an apocryphal incident of World War I. In a shellhole during a bombardment, said Frankl, were caught, by accident, two men. One was an Austrian private; the other was a Prussian colonel. During a temporary pause in the shelling, the Prussian asked the private, "Are you frightened?" The Austrian replied, "Yes, I am terrified." The officer then said, "That shows the superiority of race and training. I am not frightened." The Austrian soldier answered, "It shows the difference, but not the superiority. If you were one half as frightened as I am, you would have run away long ago!"

————•◆•————

One useful way that we have been developing to look at the process of psychotherapy is that the therapist helps the patient find a new story with which to explain his life and feelings and thus make them more personally acceptable and less painful.

One patient in her twenties blamed her "nervous breakdown" on her parents' divorce and on the two "bad people" (her mother's boyfriend and her father's girlfriend) who kept her parents from getting together again. It was "their fault" that she had her symptoms and was suffering so much from them. The therapist helped her to the concept that she was having the symptoms so that the parents would be closer together (they spent much time talking and conferring about her and shared the cost of the psychotherapy). No longer, with this interpretation, was she the helpless victim of someone else who was causing the problem and responsible for her pain. She was in charge and, feeling more in control of her symptoms, "decided" not to have them anymore. (Anne Appelbaum, personal communication, 1994.)

Which story was true? Both were interpretations of the situation and equally true. The second was "better" in that, in using it, her pain was less, she could function more effectively, and she was released from stasis to grow in new directions.

Which story was the true one in the movie *Rashomon*? All and none. Each story was a good explanation for a given person.

In science a "truth" about a problem, its solution, is one that makes our curiosity falter. The same principle holds true in life.

In his *Memories, Dreams and Reflections*, Jung wrote:

> I can only make direct statements and "tell stories," whether or not the stories are "true" is not the problem.

> The only question is whether or not what I tell is *my* fable, *my* truth. [quoted in West 1984, p. x]

A recent important study of the concept of "mental health" states:

> We treat early memories like projective tests. That is, we do not assume that the memories are accurate accounts of past events. Rather we see these as sources of information about how a person construes, organizes, and presents his experiences—that is, as a source of information about the "lenses" through which a person sees himself and his world. [Shedler et al. 1993, p. 118]

From this viewpoint, one can see why the "fads" in psychotherapy (alcoholic parents, sexual abuse, multiple-personality syndrome, etc.) are so popular. They offer a new and ready-made story that removes guilt, makes the problem someone else's fault, and accounts for the situation. Both therapist and patient tend to find it attractive and easy to take a story ready-made off the rack and not have to go to the trouble and difficulty of designing an individual one for each new patient. The reason that these "cures" tend to be so temporary is that they do not really "fit" the patient but only approximate his needs. Most patients helped by one of these ready-mades or others like them (as traumas incurred in a previous life) are back looking for another magic answer within the next few years. Each story, to be effective over any length of time, must be highly individual.

Martin Buber writes somewhere that each person must consider three things: Where did you come from? Where are you going? To whom will you have to render accounts? It may well be that each person's story must include these three elements.

Certainly each story must have the person as the center—as the protagonist. It defines, designs, and explains his feelings and behavior.

Because of the fact that we have believed that in the therapeutic process we are searching for the truth ("And the truth shall make you free!"), we have devoted very little time and effort to a major question: "Under what conditions will the patient be able to give up his old story and emotionally accept a new one?" We know a little, a few of the parameters involved here. It helps if the patient feels loved, cared for, and understood by the therapist. It often helps if the patient is in a good deal of pain and the old story is therefore no longer tenable. It helps if the patient comes to therapy committed to change and growth as a few of our patients do and not, as the majority, simply looking for new techniques to manipulate others more effectively. Beyond this, we know little and have much to learn.

4

THE PRACTICE
OF PSYCHOTHERAPY

Every philosophy and every psychology reflects the period in which it was written. (This certainly includes the present work.) In our era we look to the possibilities of the future to define the present, not to the events of the past. One problem with traditional psychotherapy is that it has been largely out of touch with this basic viewpoint of our age. It has attempted to define the present in terms of past events rather than in terms of the ever-opening future.

Modern man typically sets his life goals on what is to come and displays an attitude quite the converse of earlier days. Ancient Egypt, Greece, Rome, the vast Asiatic civilizations, even the Renaissance, did not look ahead for the ideals and inspirations of their existence, but sought them in their origins, in their ancient glories, their fabled heroes, their pristine virtues, real or

fancied. Unlike modern man who dreams of the world
he will make, premodern man dreamt of the world he
had left. [Heilbroner 1959, p. 18]

It is not only the orientation of our age that makes
it important for therapy to be focused on goal and action—it is also the way our minds function. In his brilliant book *How We Think*, John Dewey (1910) said, *"The
problem fixes the end of thought and the end controls the
process of thinking"* (p. 12; italics his).

A psychotherapy oriented to the past ignores this
crucial point and slows the processes of curing and
healing to a very great degree.

However, let us not go overboard on this. There *is* a
baby in this bathwater! Exploration of the past *is absolutely necessary* in order that the patient understand how
and why he defined the situation so that it wound up
as a problem. Until we understand what our behavior
is and why we do it, it is not only difficult to change,
but the new change is often unstable. In working with
cancer patients where the goal was to increase the activity of the immune system and bring this resource to
the aid of the medical protocol, it was absolutely necessary to first change the patterns of being, relating, and
creativity so that they more accurately reflected the
unique nature of *this* person. A second step, however,
often overlapping with the first, was to help the patient
comprehend how and why they had not done this in
their lives before. Unless the second step was taken, the
first tended to be unstable and collapse under the
stresses of everyday life. It should also be stated here
that once the first step had been taken, it was very often
far easier to take the second than our usual experience
in psychotherapy would lead us to expect. It was as if

much of the anxiety connected with bringing this understanding to consciousness had been drained off in the previous changes.

It is well known and accepted today that any specific idea or belief, accepted by a person (or group), rests firmly implanted in the overall system of philosophy (particularly metaphysics and ethics) of the person. This very strongly includes the person's view of him- or herself, what a good person is, the friendliness or unfriendliness of the universe, and so forth. For a fuller discussion of this, see *The Social Compulsions of Ideas* by Gerard De Gre (1985) or Brand Blanshard's (1939) *The Nature of Thought*.

This, of course, is why psychotherapy is a difficult process. In order to make a stable change in his ideas about himself and how to live his life, the patient must shift the entire fabric of his belief system. This is, to put it mildly, not easy. We humans find it very hard to change. In the unfortunately often true words of W. H. Auden (1947):

> We would rather be ruined than change,
> We would rather die in our dread,
> Than climb the cross of the moment
> And let our illusions die. [p. 363]

With the best will and intent in the world, it is hard to change. From 2,500 years' experience with the esoteric schools, 100 years' experience with psychotherapy, and 50 years' experience with New Age methods, we have learned this: It takes a commitment on the part of the patient, caring and modeling on the part of the therapist, a goal orientation and a therapeutic alliance, to make it possible for psychotherapy to lead to the kind of change that heals the patient. In particular, it takes

the kind of respect and caring on the part of the therapist that leads him or her to relate to *this* patient as an
individual and not as a DSM classification.

In designing a psychotherapy for the twenty-first
century, we must design one that is relevant to *this* period of history. Attempts to design a universal psychotherapy are far beyond our possibilities. (Karl Popper
once wrote, "There is no history of mankind, there is
only an indefinite number of histories of all kinds of
aspects of human life.") The basic statement of the
schools of social work has been "Take the patient where
he is. . . ." Any hopefully useful psychotherapeutic approach must take humanity where it is.

Although stressed much earlier by such figures as
Kurt Goldstein, Otto Rank, and Trigant Burrow, the
concept of looking forward rather than backward in
psychotherapy was made a center of the approach of
Viktor Frankl in his *Logotherapy.* ("In my end is my
beginning," says T. S. Eliot in *Four Quartets.*) A psychotherapy of the present era with its stress on goals and
the future will use this orientation to a greater degree
than we traditionally have.

An important aspect of the new approach is the call
to action—the recognition that talk reinforced by positive action is far more influential in the patient's life
than talk alone. This is true even if the talk is accom-
panied by strong feelings. In this we have come a long
distance and made an almost complete about-face from
the early days of psychoanalysis and the therapies de-
rivative from it in the first half of the century. In those
days the therapist would strongly urge the patient *not*
to make any changes in his life or any decisions until
the analysis was finished. The theory behind this was
that the patient was incapable of making rational decisions until the analysis was complete; up to that point

he would be in the grip of unconscious determinants, and any decision would be neurotic.

Today, rather than forbidding the patient to take any real actions in his life until the therapeutic process is complete (whatever *that* means), we measure the success and movement of the therapy by the new and action-oriented decisions the patient makes, the changes he initiates in his life. We say, with Goethe, "Whatever you can do, or dream you can do, begin it. Boldness has genius, power and magic in it."

We have learned that it is action and making choices in the real world that strengthens the person and gives them the ability to make other decisions and to act in their own growth and interest. We have learned the truth of the old statement of Democritis of Abdera that "speech is the shadow of action." For growth, we need the substance, not the shadow.

Some years ago I took a friend to the hospital for an angiogram. This is a procedure in which a thin metal tube is inserted into an artery in the groin, slowly worked upward until the tip enters the heart. Then a dye is pumped through the tube and the action of the heart photographed. It is not a pleasant procedure at best and can be very painful, but it is generally not as bad as the description makes people feel it will be. My friend was terrified. She was admitted to the hospital and given a bed. She was very frightened and lay there extremely tense and smoking cigarette after cigarette. Discussion of her feelings and of the situation did nothing to relieve her anxiety. Finally I said to her, "I am going outside the door and closing it behind me. For the next ten minutes no one, and I mean no one, is going to come in here. During that time, you decide whether or not you want to have this procedure. Your clothes are in the closet. If you decide you do not want it, get dressed and I will take you out of here. We will just walk out and I hope they try to stop us because then we will sue them for kidnapping, assault and battery, and what not and wind up rich!" I went out, guarded the door for ten minutes, and then went back in. She was still in bed but clearly much more relaxed. She said, "I still don't like it, but *I* have decided to do the procedure. I can handle it now." The procedure went off successfully.

We try to help the patient move toward action because action is a crucial element in change. The individual marks his own changes to himself by the new actions this leads to. He learns how he has changed by what he does that he did not do before. Also, each new action helps him to new developments and to the capability for new actions. Just talk has an unfortunate tendency to just lead to more talk. This is one reason that the long analyses of the past, often year after year, lasted so long and so often showed so little results.

There is an old Chinese proverb, "I hear, and I forget. I see, and I remember. I do, and I understand."

The search for wisdom in the East and for insight in the West lead to pretty much the same halfway place. Both leave you with a feeling of accomplishment and control and not very much real progress. Both insight and Eastern wisdom are the perception of doors out of human traps and toward human growth. Once we see and comprehend the "doors," we are ready for the hard work of walking toward and through them. Similarly to drugs like LSD or Mescaline, they place you high on a mountain from which you can see the promised land across the intervening desert. You can either stay up on the mountain or climb down to begin the long slog across the desert now that you know your destination, the direction, and you are free of past inhibitions against walking.

As Tony Schwartz (1995) has shown in his excellent and important *What Really Matters: The Search for Wisdom in America,* the search for wisdom is only the first step toward the goal. It leads to the possibility of being able to work for your own advancement.

As I can only see my face in a mirror (although I can visualize it as ugly or handsome, familial or foreign, in my imagination and feelings), I can only see my interior life in the mirror of my actions. To the degree my actions have shape, coherence, direction, and discipline, so does my inner life. To the degree my actions reflect in pace, direction, and substance what I really am, I am in harmony with myself.

My activities are necessary (except for rest periods) for my mental and physical health. Without goal directed and organized activity, the inner life decays; the bodily defenses function at a lower level. This is why the greatest killer in Western civilization is not heart disease or cancer but retirement. When it is "retirement from," not "retirement to" (to use John Dewey's terms), this is true, as there is no more goal around which to organize our activities. It is very rare that "to rest and play golf" is an adequate center for our lives.

Crucial to all of this is *harmony,* harmony between what one is built for and what one does. Finding out what is one's true nature is often a long and hard task, frequently with much deadwood (in the shape of misconceptions) to be cleared away. Indeed, this often takes a large part of the time required for psychotherapy. However, the game is well worth the candle. It is this harmony between our nature and our ways of being, relating, creating, that is an essential part of healing. The therapist who does not keep this clearly in mind is constantly in danger of losing the path and also of trivializing the process. If you are a therapist, this might be a good time to think back on the many times that this has happened with you, in both your professional practice and your personal therapy.

In this call to action, we return also to the Western spiritual tradition. Insofar as spiritual development is concerned, in the West we have always been more concerned with what you did than with how you felt. In *The Ascent to Mount Carmel*, St. John of the Cross wrote, "If you were in an ecstasy as deep as that of St. Paul, and a sick man needed a cup of soup, it were better for you that you returned from the ecstasy and brought him the soup for love's sake." Martin Buber writes that in the hasidic tradition, "Man cannot love God without loving the world." Henry IV, Emperor of Germany, wanted to join the monks of the Abbey of Verdun. They refused him, saying that his job was to rule Germany. After strong political pressure, however, they accepted him and immediately after he had taken the vow of obedience, assigned him his first—and permanent— job: to go back and rule Germany. In the West, the path to beyond the world leads through the world, and this is the hardest and most important part of it.

In this new insight into psychotherapy that we have been developing, action is the key to the spiritual life. We have found that as individuals search for their own unique and specific ways to sing their own song, beat out the individual, one-of-a-kind music of their personality, they come upon a need to express in work, in a particular kind of work, their concern with more than themselves or their family. This need appears in nearly all persons with whom we have worked from this new viewpoint. I have ex-patients who spend an evening a week or more working with ecology organizations, peace organizations, Big Brother and Big Sister programs, literacy programs, and a wide variety of others.

They say things like, "It feeds a part of me that I did not know was there and did not know was hungry."

In Latin the words "to live" and "to be among men" (*inter homines esse*) or "to die" and "to cease to be among men" (*inter homenes esse desinere*) are synonyms (Arendt 1958, p. 7).

It is important that the impetus for this work comes from selfish needs and the discovery that one is doing this for one's own sake and not for a general belief that one is only a good person if one is a do-gooder and altruistic. We all know many people, often pretty disturbed people, who have always been for other people first and have spent their lives taking care of others. As Christopher Pilkington, the Canon of Wells Cathedral in England once remarked, "And you can always tell the others by the hunted look in their eyes!"

In the last analysis, we are a social species. Our inner life is built on our relationships with others. The primary goal of psychotherapy is the upgrading of our relationship with ourselves, with others, and with the general cosmos of which we all know that somehow we are a part. To improve one of these alone builds a house on sand. The improvement cannot stand; it will fall when the first wind blows. Unless the therapist has clearly in mind that these three are so interconnected and interwoven that what happens to one ultimately either undermines or strengthens the other two, the therapy process will be badly handicapped. We do not and cannot flourish, or even usually stay alive, in isolation. If a great primate expert like Wolfgang Köhler could say, "A solitary chimpanzee is not a chimpanzee," what can we say about human beings? Kurt Goldstein once remarked in this context, "The whole idea of self should be abandoned. There is no such thing as self in isolation. Self only exists in relation to others."

Here the difference between curing and healing becomes clear. The therapist may help cure a specific problem and reduce the pain from it. To heal means to so upgrade the person's life in all three areas—the relationship with self, with others, and with the cosmos—that the person can cure the problem him- or herself and be in a strong enough position and with an attitude so that he or she is most likely to be able to cure other specific problems as they arise and to keep on growing to be more unique, more individual, and more related to others in the specific ways that suit the person's particular personality constellation.

There is no "right" way to relate to others. The chef and the waiter do it in different ways, the book author and the stage performer likewise. The hermit may relate deeply and passionately to others and to the universe while physically alone in a cave in the wilderness. (Thomas Merton wrote, "The Western monk retires to the world, not from it" from his silent Trappist monastery.)

Each of us needs a particular balance of solitude and relationship. For helping the patient search for the right balance for him- or herself is a crucial part of therapy. The search makes it plain, on the most basic level, that the therapist *respects* the real individuality of the patient and thus helps the patient accept and respect him- or herself.

Parallel to this is the way that many of us are learning (following the lead of the psychiatrist Herbert Spiegel) to help patients realize whether their locus of control is inner or outer, whether they are primarily responsive to cues from the inner environment or the outer environment, and accept this as a legitimate fact. These facts, the percentages of solitude and of relationship a person needs and the locus of control, are not things to be adjusted so as to fit the patterns approved of by society or held by the therapist to be right because they are his own. (The exception is, of course, where there is a strong neurotic element affecting these traits as when, for example, a person fears that he will harm others if he gets close to them and so avoids closer contact. Or the opposite, when the person is so afraid of his own inner thoughts that he must be constantly relating, must "flee into reality" and avoid all solitude. Here psychotherapy should the analyze and explore until the person can get past the neurosis and find those balances right for him and learn to respect them and accept them because they are his.) The acceptance of the self is crucial to all healthy growth and becoming, and to healthy relationships to others and to the cosmos in general.

When the patient stops asking, "What is the best way to live?" (a question akin to asking a chess master, "What is the best move?") and starts asking, "At this time in my individual one-of-a-kind journey through life, how best should I act to increase my flourishing?" we are well on the road to healing.

———•◆•———

Healing is a continuous process that is never finished. It partially consists of living with an attitude that there is always more and that there is no end to growth. One's relationship with the self, with others, and with the cosmos always need deepening and expanding. The path has no ending, but to become fixed on one spot on it is like the psychoanalytic concept of being fixated at one stage of growth and not being able to continue with one's development. There is always more room to grow, more steps on the path.

This point is illustrated by an old legend. In the

Bible, in Psalm 56, it says that God preserves all your tears. The legend, which attempts to explain this strange statement and say why God would do this, states that when you arrive in Heaven, you are confused and do not know how to behave. You are given a bottle containing all the tears that you shed while you lived on earth. The task that goes with this gift is that you must find the best possible use for them. Somewhere in the world is a barren spot of ground in which the dry seeds cannot sprout for lack of moisture. Or a child who is dying of thirst. Or a person who has been burned and needs moisture on the burned flesh. Or a baby whose mother can give him no milk since she is lost in the desert and has no water. You must search the entire earth until you find what you consider the best possible use for this small bottle of tears and use it in the place where you believe it will have most effect. When you have completed the task and bring back the empty bottle, you find that you now know how to behave in Heaven.

The therapist should be as concerned with his or her own continuous growth as he is with that of the patient. In the old Hassidic teaching story, the wise man was arrested by the Inquisition and interrogated. As a test he was asked why God said to Adam in the Garden, "Where art thou?" "Did not," asked the inquisitor, "God always know where each person was? Why did he have to ask?" The seer replied that the scriptures were not just history but applied to each person at all times. Their lesson was always *now*. "Each person has an allotted span of life in which to accomplish his task of becoming. At each moment God asks, 'Where art thou? How are *you* progressing on your journey?'"

The therapist can never know what the patient *should* become. Each person is a mystery with his or her potential hidden in the future. As each period of time passes, each new petal unfolds from the bud, new possibilities exist. What we *can* say is whether the patient is growing, changing, becoming more unique and individual. Surely there must be plateaus where we gather our strength, where we integrate what we have learned and digest our experiences. But then we resume our growth if we are healed and have seen ourselves as an integrated whole that is dynamic and vital. There is no bottom to anything serious—to our ability to love, to appreciate beauty, to feel more at home in the cosmos with ourselves and with others, to act effectively, to know our home on this planet, and to care for it, for our shipmates, and for ourselves. There is always room for growth and change in our own direction and the ability to get more out of life.

Without knowing the specific goal for each patient (or for himself) the therapist can always say, "Where art thou?" The question is one of movement, not goal.

————•◆•————

One of the shibboleths that we have gradually abandoned in the last few years has been the basic metaphor of homeostasis or equilibrium for mental health. For this we have substituted a goal-directed striving in which both the goal and the method of striving has been chosen by the patient as an expression of his own uniqueness. Viktor Frankl (1959) expressed this change as follows:

> What man actually needs is not a tensionless state but rather the striving and struggling for a worthwhile goal, a freely chosen task. What he needs is not the discharge of tension at any cost, but the call of a potential meaning waiting to be fulfilled by him. [p. 127]

Another basic concept of psychotherapy that we have given up is the question of whether human beings are, at bottom, good and/or evil. The idea of human beings being basically carnivores whose "natural" life was "nasty, brutish, short, and cold," as Hobbes and Freud thought, or basically loving and altruistic, as Rousseau and Rogers believed, was an underlying problem in the social sciences. (The third alternative widely accepted—that they were *tabula rasas*, blank tablets that could develop into anything—was implicitly followed particularly by those of Behaviorist orientations.) Although there was very little experimental work in this area (see Appendix I for one exception), the answer accepted by the particular individual underlay many psychotherapeutic techniques and personality theories. Verbalized or unverbalized questions, however, that are valid in one period are irrelevant to the way the universe is construed in another. We are no longer interested in questions raised by the three-day seminars given by St. Thomas Aquinas on such subjects as "Do angels know the future?" Nor in the long arguments at the court of Louis XIV on whether two "perfect" painters, working with the same model, would paint identical pictures. Nor in the nature-nurture controversy so widely discussed thirty years ago. Nor in the question of the basic nature of *Homo Sapiens* (or *Homo Faber* or *Homo Ludens* or whatever else you might care to call our comic and tragic species). We have decided, without any particular discussion of the matter, that human beings are so complicated and complex, are so capable of so much and so little, that they are not simply basically good or evil. In the words of T. H. White (1977), "To disbelieve in original sin does not mean that you must believe in original virtue" (p. 6).

———•◆•———

One of the strangest developments in psychotherapy (and in particular in the Human Potential groups involved in therapy) has been the concept of the "wounded healer." In this concept, a therapist says, in effect or openly, "I am neurotic and therefore a better psychotherapist because I understand what it feels like to be a neurotic." I have never heard one of these people (those who use this concept) say, "I was wounded and neurotic and fought and struggled my way out of it, and therefore I am a better psychotherapist because I understand and comprehend what it means to struggle to be healthy." The emphasis in this concept is on being sick, not on attaining the self. The neurosis is turned into a justification for the person to be a· psychotherapist. Surely this is one of the neatest bits of rationalization in history. It also often serves as a justification for the therapist not to have personal psychotherapy and not to work actively toward his or her own growth.

Edgar Allan Poe may have been right in his "Dr. Tarr and Professor Fether" when he said that the patients and doctors in his mythical insane asylum were interchangeable and that the only way one could tell them apart was by the clothes they wore and who carried the keys. However, we have come a long way since Poe's day. We are no longer concerned primarily with the illness and its description, but with the individual's resources to grow and how we can permit and encourage this.

For the "wounded healer" to say, "I was sick and worked very hard and learned about growth and movement from it" is one thing. To say, "I am a sickie and therefore can help other sickies better" is something else.

————•◆•————

Respect for the patient means acceptance of the way that the patient construes the world (unless the construction is getting them into unnecessary trouble and causing problems that cannot be dealt with in that construction). It means acceptance, but not patronizing. The fine line here is demonstrated by an incident that occurred some years ago when George Engel was leading a group of interns, residents, and medical students on rounds in a hospital. (Engel is the man who wrote that great classic of holistic medicine, "The Need for a New Biomedical Model.") An older woman with a severe brain cancer asked him, "Doctor, do I have a male or a female cancer?" Engel very seriously asked her what the difference was between them. She replied that you died with great pain of a male cancer, but with no pain from a female cancer. Engel took her chart and examined it with great care, reading each page slowly to himself. He then told her that there was no question but that her cancer was female.

After rounds, in the discussion in the conference room, the students protested vigorously to Engel. They said that the patient was living in a fantasy and that she had a right to the full and accurate diagnosis in the proper medical terms. Most of them were too young and inexperienced to understand that telling the woman that her metaphor for the situation was incorrect and invalid and that the doctor's was the correct one would have been, in this case, destructive. It would only have increased the woman's concern and confusion. And, in all probability, have increased the likelihood of pain from her cancer.

Another example of the need and value of accepting the patient's frame of reference rather than by immediately responding with our own is shown in an incident that occurred a number of years ago when Freda Fromm-Reichmann was taking a group on rounds in Chestnut Lodge. A woman was standing at the foot of her bed as we approached. Fromm-Reichmann said to her, "How are you today, Mary?" The woman responded, to the shock of all of us, by shooting out her clenched fist, palm upward with the middle finger extended in the air toward her. This was the classic "giving the finger" if we had ever seen it, and we all responded appropriately except Fromm-Reichmann, who looked at the extended hand with the single finger standing in the air and said softly, "So lonely?" The woman responded by nodding her head in agreement with a profoundly sad expression on her face. Fromm-Reichmann put her arm around the woman's shoulders and led her back to sitting on the bed saying, "I will be back here in exactly one hour and then we will talk. Will that be all right?" The woman again nodded her head yes, and the group proceeded on rounds.

As we gain more and more respect for the patient and his ability to grow in his own direction once given the opportunity, we can confidently expect that the influence of fads in therapeutic circles will become less. What has happened in the past—and is still going on— is that as we try to direct the patient into the "correct" path, we sometimes find ourselves directing him into the path of the latest fad. Since this provides an acceptable answer to the problem of what caused the patient's pain, anxiety, and/or guilt, a new metaphor that is socially acceptable and blames everything on someone or something else is frequently accepted by the patient with enthusiasm, and generally a host of highly detailed screen memories emerges to support it. Sometimes a problem is cured in this way; healing rarely if ever occurs.

A recent major fad was that all the patient's problems came from having alcoholic parents. When evidence showed that specific parents were not drinkers,
then everything was explained on the basis that they had
the personalities of alcoholics. This explained everything, and the patient could relax with the knowledge
that nothing he had done or felt was his fault or responsibility but caused by those awful drunks he had for
parents and what they had done to him in typical alcoholic fashion.

Certainly there *were* alcoholic parents who damaged
their children. But there were far less of them than were
reported and believed in and remembered when the fad
was at its height. Presently the fad died down and many
of those who had firmly and deeply believed that they
had solved all their problems went forth again in search
of another cause. And one quickly appeared. Patients
had been sexually abused by their parents. Many therapists quickly grabbed this idea. After all, it reinforced
their belief that *someone* must be to blame so they could
reduce their patient's guilt. Very often, with a little
adroit questioning and subtle or not so subtle interpretations, the most amazing details and clear memories
were suddenly conscious. A large number of families
in which nothing of this sort had ever actually occurred
were badly damaged by not-very-bright therapists who,
now that the children-of-alcoholic-parents fad had lost
its zing and popularity, were looking to see whether
their patients had been sexually abused and, in the
search, produced the evidence they were looking for.
After all, if the patients of Adlerian therapists came up
with dreams about the search for power, and the patients of Rankian therapists came up with dreams
about the birth process, and those of Jungian therapists dreams full of archetypical figure, and those of

Freudian therapists—but you get the idea. Then why not conscious memories of being sexually abused by the patients of therapists who were oriented in that direction? In any case, it certainly happened.

What the next fad will be, I do not know. As I write this in February 1994, I rather suspect it will be a very large number of patients who begin in therapy to remember having been picked up by aliens in a flying saucer, given a tour of the ship, a meal, a physical examination, and whatever else, and then having the whole thing hypnotically repressed and all their troubles coming from this experience. When you point out that their psychological problems predated the date of the recalled event, this will have no more effect than it did when it was pointed out during the alcoholic parents fad that their parents did not drink.

Let us be clear. There *were* children badly mistreated by alcoholic parents and children who were sexually abused and, for all I know, people who were picked up by ETs and the experience hypnotically repressed. Although there apparently were more of the first two classes (at any rate) than we had suspected, there were certainly far less than were reported. Similarly, when the fad of being a multiple personality and that accounting for all your troubles was at its height, there certainly were some real multiple personalities around, but, equally certainly, there were far less than was reported.

The pressure on the therapist to go along with *and believe in* the fad of the moment is often very heavy. It seems to be the most "modern" and new knowledge, and we are really up with the times and ahead of all the other stick-in-the-muds around us. Also, it brings in a new group of patients who have read about this in the newspapers (even as we have) and tell their friends that you are the newest expert in the field. Above all, however, is the fact that it proves itself valid. As we search to see if our patients have had this, the evidence is forthcoming. The more we search, the more detail is produced, and the patient certainly acts and feels as if it were real. We forget how effectively the unconscious, given proper motivation, can act as playwright, producer and director and bring forth the most amazing and detailed plays about something that never happened. Children are particularly susceptible to this. We have all by now seen enough examples where therapists by asking such questions as "Did he touch you there?" and "Did it hurt when he touched you there?" produced detailed scripts and highly emotional stories about childhood rape, satanism, burying of elephants in the back yard, witnessing the drowning of the other children at sea (this last in a state in the middle of the country that the child had never left), and so forth. Children may be the most vulnerable, but adults are pretty susceptible too. It is truly amazing how many multiple personalities there were in the general patient population when the fad was at its height and how few there were a couple of years later.

The problem, of course, is not a new one or restricted to psychotherapists alone. Over 2,500 years ago, Heracleitus wrote, "A foolish man is apt to be in a flutter over every theory." With so many new theories appearing every day, waiting ten or fifteen years to see if one has fruitfulness before embracing it may not be a bad idea.

Shifting the focus of our respect from our theories (and the latest information about human beings) to our patient's ability to grow in healthy directions given a chance, should ease this tendency to a considerable degree.

A few years ago I was in the German city of Heidelberg. I was talking with a group of young people, all of whom had been born at the beginning of World War II or shortly before. All were psychologists or psychiatrists. I had noticed that all of the lovely city was built of orange brick except for two buildings and two arches of the bridges over the river, which were of a yellower color. I asked about this, and all agreed that it was due to the Allied bombing of the city. When I told them that Heidelberg had never been bombed, they were furious. Not only had their parents described the bombing in detail, but all the older ones remembered it. They told me how they had huddled in the shelters, described the roar of the bombs, the frightened coming out afterward, not sure if it was really over for now, the dust settling from the explosions, anxious inquiries to find out if friends or family members had been killed, and so forth.

The details were completely convincing and consistent. When I insisted that they had not been bombed, they angrily asked me if I had been with the Allied Air Command during the war or if I was a specialist in military history. I replied no but that I was a psychologist. We made a bet of twenty marks (about ten dollars) and went in search of a history of the war in Heidelberg. The book we found said that Heidelberg had never been bombed, but that at the end of the war, the mayor, obeying Hitler's scorched earth policy, had started to destroy the city and had blown up two buildings and two arches over the river when the citizens caught up with him and killed him.

The German young people asked me how I had known this. I answered that to Americans and to the English people, Heidelberg is not Germany. It is "The Student Prince" and "Gaudeamus Igatur." Many of the teachers of my teachers in psychology and other fields had gone to Heidelberg to study, and there were wall hangings in many of their homes with pictures of *Alte*

Heidelberg Du Shön on them. (For example, William James and G. Stanley Hall spent the summer of 1880 there together and, in long discussions, laid down the future of psychology for many years to come.) Any American or British general who ordered or permitted the bombing of Heidelberg would have been retired the next day or worse.

The point is not how clever I was or how much people enjoy Sigmund Romberg! The point is that the German young people remembered in detail and with appropriate emotion an event that did not exist and that had never happened. How many of our patients do the same thing under the proper stimulation?

———•◆•———

No therapist, of course, can reasonably be expected to be able to relate in many ways to his or her patients or to be able to be a part of the environments that some patients will need in order to grow and flourish most effectively. What do we do in these circumstances—when a specific patient who comes into the office turns out to need an environment we cannot provide effectively?

The obvious answer is that we should refer these patients to a therapist who *can* provide what is needed. However, this runs into a financial question. We make our living from the number of patients we have. Unfortunately, psychotherapy today is more often a business profession than a service profession. We have to make decisions in specific cases as to where our self-interest and financial problems leave off and where the best interest of the patient begins. Unfortunately, this is a marvelous area for rationalizations, and we therapists are no more immune from this than the rest of the population.

Very often we are aware that there is another therapist down the block who would be better for this patient than we are. However, we have bills to meet. What do we do then?

There is, we all know, a contract made immediately when a patient comes into our office. On the patient's side the contract reads, "I will do my best to be honest and talk about what is important to me." On the therapist's side it reads, "I will do my best to be helpful to you." What then do we do if being most helpful to the patient means to refer him to someone else? Mostly, of course, we simply repress the fact that any problem exists and start checking schedules with the patient to see at what hour we can make a regular series of appointments.

In terms of the existence of this contract, it is clearly a highly immoral act to refer a patient to someone else because they are a friend, or starting a new practice and we wish to help them, or for any reason except the one that we have thought about the patient and, in our careful opinion, this is the best therapist available for him. Referring to a specific therapist for any reason but this is a violation of our contract and our ethics.

The one area where, thank God, we mostly have learned that it is necessary to refer is when we find that we cannot really care for a prospective patient. When we know that we will not be able to love him or her. Then we do generally refer.

When, in the 1940s I was being trained as a psychotherapist in the Veterans Administration, at Cushing Hospital, an entirely different approach was standard policy. If you did not like a patient or were known to be unable to empathize or relate to a particular kind of patient, then you were assigned the patient or a heavy load of the syndrome with which you could not relate. The idea was that this would help the therapist grow. At the time and now it has seemed to me that this was a concern (mistaken or not) with the therapist and a lack of concern with the patient. Fortunately this type of policy is (I hope) long in the past.

The idea that a therapist could work effectively with a patient he could not really like and care for derives from the old idea that therapy is essentially a mechanistic procedure in which, if you said the right things in the right tone and the right moment, you could cure the patient, if he were curable. This concept reached its highest point in orthodox psychoanalysis and even there was never accepted by the best of the analysts. In the 1940s, Otto Fenichel, at that time the (unofficial) *Agitprop* of the analytic movement, was imploring the analysts he was training to be "warm, open, meet the patient as a human being." Eventually it was generally realized that not relating as a person to the patient but treating him in a mechanistic way, at best, taught the patient to regard himself as an object to be manipulated. In this way, one might cure a symptom but could not usually heal the person. And very often did long-term damage to his personality.

———•◆•———

It is difficult, as a psychotherapist, constantly to remain at one's highest peak of alertness and being-with-the-orientation. Staying on the *qui-vive* as each new patient comes in, being fully alert and *engagé*, related, is far from easy. The fine edge dulls, we begin, not noticing it, to coast, to depend on our training and commitment, trusting in these to call us to full attention if anything happens that demands this of us. Like an automobile driver on a long trip, we go on automatic, rousing to full alert only when the unusual or the dangerous occurs.

Presently, as we go on in our practice, and particularly toward the end of the day (and more so at the end of the week), we coast more and more without being aware of it.

The Director of the Helen Dowling Institute for Biopsychosocial Medicine in Rotterdam is a remarkable man named Marco de Vries. He trains psychotherapists there (among other duties) and once when I was visiting allowed me to take one of his training methods. This is a computer program in which the computer acts as the therapist. The screen would show the computer's side of the interchange and I would type in my (the patient's) responses.

It was one of the most startling and shocking experiences I have ever had. Over and over the screen replied to my typed comments with a phrase or comment I had frequently used myself when functioning as a therapist in a real situation. For example, the computer asked me how I felt now. I replied I was tense but not sure of the reason. The computer wrote, "Let's ask your inner child about this." I typed in anger that I wasn't going to talk to a damned machine. The computer wrote, "I thought we were talking about you, not about me."

After a half hour of this, I got up from the console, walked over to the nearest bar, and had three Ginevra gins in succession. Ordinarily I am not a drinking man, but the lesson had been so sharp and painful that, for the moment, I changed my habits. The machine had behaved exactly as I did when I was "coasting," when I was not completely engaged with the patient and the commitment to his growth. I knew then that if I ever allowed myself to coast again, I would know that I was failing the patient and myself.

A few years later I was doing a demonstration of a first interview with a group of therapists. One commented in the discussion afterward that he had been struck by how *hard* I worked all through the session, that I seemed constantly to be on high alert. I said I had had a good teacher for this by the name of Marco de Vries but did not add that it was Marco's computer program that really nailed home the lesson.

———•———

Since Plato and later Descartes taught us that reason should rule and Freud convinced us that the way to fullest health was to remember as much as possible of the traumatic events and interpretations of our past, we have had the general belief that the more of the past that was remembered, the better off the person was psychologically. This is certainly true for some of our patients, but it is far from a universal rule. There *is* an unconscious and it has a purpose, and meaning and part of this is that part of our past belongs in it. Nature makes no luxuries, and the idea that *everything* should be accessible to consciousness and that the unconscious should be drained as far as possible is an interesting one, but not one that bears close scrutiny. Forgetting is as important to our health as remembering. (How many women would have a second child if the experience of bearing the first was not quickly repressed?)

To illustrate this by something of a *reductio ad absurdam*, do you really think that things would be improved if one made the unconscious conscious of Mozart, Rodin, Dali (arguably the greatest religious painter since the Renaissance), or Tennyson?

Another related belief that we are reexamining and limiting in its application is the idea that the communication of ideas and feelings and beliefs is necessarily positive. There is no question that this is often valid, but we are beginning to see that often it is not. To use the artist as an example again, there are times during the creative experience when communication has a negative effect. As ideas and concepts are coming to clarity, to "jelling," it is often best if the creative person holds them without communicating anything about them to others or even showing them to another person. The time for discussion is after they have jelled and can maintain their special quality against the impact of other opinions. Some things should be communicated, some not.

Another widely accepted shibboleth that has not stood the test of time is that the durability of the cure is related to the length of treatment. The source of this idea was originally the belief that unless you had a full psychoanalysis, all positive changes were transitory since you had not fully dealt with the original cause—the trauma of the fixation at an early stage of development. However, by now we have all seen too many exceptions at both ends of the treatment time scale to have any belief in this idea.

We have, in the field of psychotherapy, frequently used the analogy of the parent–child relationship. This has been done under two separate aspects that have often become confused. The first is when the patient acts out certain attitudes and relationship techniques with the therapist as if the therapist *were* the parent. This aspect, whether one calls it "transference" or "parataxic distortion" or whatnot, is certainly something that sometimes happens and is grist for the therapeutic process. It is to be analyzed or otherwise dealt with. It was originally discovered by Freud in the very early part of the century and developed by him and his followers (notably by August Aichorn, "The Hawk of the Transference") in the following years. The probability of it occurring is increased to the degree that the thera-

pist becomes as invisible a personality as possible and
so serves as a screen on which these un-worked-out
needs can be projected. For *some* patients, it is an important part of the healing process.

The other aspect occurs when the therapist assumes
a parental role with its clearly implied "I know what is
best for you and how you should get there." This is an
entirely different matter, and although both patient and
therapist may accept it, and it may be a part of a curing process, it cannot be part of a healing development.
It substitutes the concept of the therapist's omniscience
for the respect for patient's ability to find his or her own
goals and path and to proceed along that path given an
environment conducive to growth.

This is one of the major problems of our field. It is
a very easy trap for both therapist and patient to fall
into. It certainly feeds the narcissism of the therapist
and makes the work of the patient of an entirely different kind. Instead of having to make the tremendous
struggle of finding out who the patient is and what is
the best way for him not only to find his real name but
to learn to live under it, he only has to be a good child
and do what he is told and he will be cured of his
problems.

One indication of the severity of the problem is given
by an incident that occurred in the 1960s. A training
analyst at the Chicago Psychoanalytic Institute was
given a large grant to investigate the early stages of the
psychoanalytic process. It was large enough so that he
could set up one-way mirrors in several of his colleagues' offices (with their knowledge and the informed
consent of their patients) and film the first dozen sessions. On examining the tapes he was shocked. They
indicated that the analyst usually made up his or her
mind in the first session as to what this particular

patient's real problem was and what a cure would be and that nothing on earth that the patient could do thereafter could shake this conviction.

The researcher edited the films to show this as clearly as possible and called a meeting of the senior staff with the question of "What are we going to do about this problem in our work?" The staff agreed about the seriousness of the problem and decided to take time while each of them would think about it. Within a few weeks, the researcher was told that first his grant was revoked and secondly that he was expelled from the institute. I might point out here that the ranking of training analyst is one of the highest that can be obtained in an analytic institute and that firing one is a very rare occurrence.

———•◆•———

It seems to me that there is a strange distortion in our present view of Sigmund Freud and his contributions to our understanding and to our society. His name is a household word in the twentieth century. All serious modern psychotherapy rests its basic structure entirely on his contributions to knowledge. Major changes have been made in a dozen fields of learning, at least, because of his ideas. It is also true that Freud's genius has been consistently underestimated and that he has been given little or no credit for most of his fundamental contributions to science.

There are five basic concepts that Freud contributed to human understanding. Four of these appear to be permanent contributions to the conceptual tools we have with which to deal with reality. It is strange that he has generally been given credit only for the one that is long outmoded. Or at least is useful only for a small and special group of patients.

Here are what I consider to be Freud's greatest contributions:

1. The concept of a scientific method by means of which we can garden each other and help individuals past the stuntings, confusions, and bindings that so restrict our capabilities and our joys. The idea of such a method was unknown before him.
2. One example of this method—psychoanalytic psychotherapy. (This is the only contribution for which Freud is generally given credit.)
3. The concept that the way to study the mind successfully is not by the method developed by physics to study objects, but a very different, yet valid, scientific method. Although this idea did not originate with Freud, he was the first to develop it to the point of real usefulness.
4. That the mind of a human being is:
   a. dynamic, endlessly flowing, and moving;
   b. complex and with various levels of consciousness and clarity constantly interacting; and
   c. comprehensible.
5. That the same method can be used to comprehend the mind and behavior of human beings and to cure the individual's psychological problems.

It is not easy from the viewpoint of the present time to realize how revolutionary these ideas were when Freud brought them to our attention. They have become accepted and are part of the framework with which we view ourselves and others. But it took one of the greatest geniuses humankind has ever produced to find, develop, and clarify them and give us the basic tools and concepts with which to explore that tremendous and unknown frontier—the mind of human beings.

In the narrow view of human beings that we use so often in the consultation room, however, we often ignore the great aspects of life in our psychotherapies. With our overconcentration on pathology, with the tendency to "explain" *everything* on the basis of childhood distortions of reality and poor parental understanding, we have left large parts of what we are outside the door. If, for example, you ask the average psychotherapist why it is that with a human history in which people have repeatedly, and in large numbers, sacrificed psychological ease and physical comfort, and sometimes even survival itself, for spiritual ends; why it is that with this knowledge the therapist pays no attention to spiritual factors in his or her therapy, you will probably get a confused look, some mutterings about this being all superstition and primitive activity we should wipe out as therapists. Further, you will probably get some suggestions about how you yourself obviously have not *worked through* your conflicts in this area, and they will be glad to see you on a regular basis (perhaps at a professional discount for the fee) in order to help you work them through.

It is not only the spiritual aspects of human beings that the modern therapist is rarely trained or equipped to deal with and to encourage and strengthen. It is also most of the other positive special aspects that make us more than animals and more than pathology. It is creativity and the love of the beautiful and of the true. It is "honor and faith and a sure intent." It is the search for the meaning of our existence. For a famous therapist to say, as one did, "Only philosophers and depressives ask, 'What is the meaning of life?'" reduces the rest of us to a lower level than we are. Whether it is worse for the scientists who study human feelings and behavior to explain these as a bunch of connected reflex arcs, or to explain them as artifacts of an advanced computer, or to explain them as a collection of reaction-formations to pathological drives (which of these is worse for the effect it has on our attitudes toward ourselves and for the future of humankind?) is a moot point indeed. All these things play a part in our being, but they no more explain them than the nuts and bolts that hold an automobile together explain and make up the automobile. Plato, long eons ago, dealt with this problem in *Meno*, and it will be necessary for psychologists to heed his words if they are ever going to succeed in their goal of helping us closer to our potential for splendor.

> There is surely a strange confusion of cause and conditions in all this," says Socrates. "It may be said, indeed, that without bones and muscles and all the other parts of the body I cannot execute my purposes. But to say that I do as I do because of them, and that this is the way in which the mind acts, and not from the choice of the best, is a very careless and idle mode of speaking. I wonder that they cannot distinguish the causes from the condition, which the many, feeling about in the dark, are always mistaking and misnaming. [Jowett translation]

It is largely for this reason—that the scientists who should be responsibly working with the spiritual and aspirational aspects of human beings have rejected this area as unworthy of them—that those people who are seeking to find these parts of themselves go so frequently to the irresponsible, kooky, and predatory groups that pretend to have knowledge and working methods to help us grow in these ways. It is psychotherapists who are responsible for the immense growth and fat bank accounts of such groups as Dianetics, Est, Mind Control, and the recent popularity of people who either hysterically believe, or else consciously pretend to be, "channelers" of discarnate spirits. (One of these—in California, of course—holds weekends of "channeling" for four hundred people at a time at four hundred dollars per person.) When psychotherapists realize that these positive aspects are real aspects of being human and that they are of tremendous importance to us, then people will not have to seek the solution to their needs at the hands of second-rate gurus, nuts, and those seeking to make personal fortunes out of these hopes and aspirations.

————◆·————

There is another useful rule of thumb to help with the evaluation of new ideas about human beings and the human condition. If the new idea is *really* new and you cannot find it stated or pretty clearly implied in literature, philosophy, or humor, it is very likely to be invalid. The best minds of the human race have been concerned about these matters and exploring them since we came out of the caves and probably before. They did not have the conceptual tools to *describe* their findings as we do and often, because of this, could not state them in *fruitful* terms, but they saw deeply and profoundly.

As an example from another field, Dionysis, the pseudo-Areopagite in the fifth century A.D., described gravity and stated that all masses of matter were attracted to each other. He did not have the mathematics, nor did he have the precise measurements of Kepler that enabled Newton over a thousand years later to prove this, but the basic idea was there. Similarly, Aristarchis of Samos, during the Hellenic period, described the movement of the earth as an ellipse around the sun.

The idea of the unconscious and its effect on our dreams was known to Plato. He did not, however, have the scientific concepts that enabled Freud to make the concept into a useful cultural tool. In spite of our natural desire to be the original pioneers and discoverers of the field of human thought and behavior, it is a pretty good general rule to say that if no one said it before, you are probably wrong!

In his definitive *History of Experimental Psychology*, Edwin G. Boring (1929) wrote, "Nothing [in psychology] that is called 'first' is ever literally first: there always turns out to have been 'anticipations'" (p. 318).

In the Hebrew tradition, there are definite requirements before one is allowed to study the mystical path, the "mysteries." There are four of these. The person must be over forty years of age so that they have had a chance to experience real life and tasted it fully instead of just hearing about it or reading about it. They must have shown the ability to survive in the world successfully so that they are going to the mystical path as a way to grow, not as a place in which to hide from the everyday world. They must have good human relationships; they must have the knowledge of another field of wisdom.

What would happen if we took these four requirements and applied them to the field of psychotherapy? Most of those now practicing would be immediately disbarred! And, in all probability, it would improve the level of work in the area by a large factor. Certainly these requirements approximate those of the wise women and men of the tribes from whom we are descended. In the medieval period, you had to be at least 35 years of age to be given the degree of master of arts in theology at the University of Paris. Thomas Aquinas was, by special dispensation of the Pope, given the degree at 31.

In this context it is of interest to note that William McDougal, one of the leading psychologists of the first half of this century, believed that psychology was a subject that should not be taught at undergraduate levels since the students were not ready for it, but it should be restricted to graduate levels. One might not completely agree with this, but there is certainly something there.

———◆·———

Certainly self-exploration and self-understanding are usually necessary parts of growth and change. We, in the West, have known this since Socrates, at any rate, and it has been a major part of our intellectual tradition long before Voltaire in his *Discourse Sur L'Homme* wrote that a person is only free to change to the degree that he understands his behavior. However, the level of consciousness and the detailed articulation of this necessary understanding varies with each person. There is no rule how much detailed knowledge a person must have in order to change nor in terms of what metaphor they must place this knowledge. In the early days of development of psychotherapy it was believed that it was necessary to have emotional catharsis of basic emotional traumas and fixations in order for there to be growth past them. Today we see that this is true for some people, true in conjunction with intellectual understanding for others, and untrue for still other people. Catharsis of a basic emotional trauma may change the overall view of the self for one person, make temporary changes and reduce stress (including stress expressed through the body) on another, have no effect on a third.

One man, John, in his forties, had had a terrible experience as a child that he had completely repressed. At 6 years of age he had been looking at a picture book while lying on the floor behind a couch in the living room of his house. His father and another man had come in and not seen him. They discussed the torture-murder they were planning for the only male (his uncle) who had ever been warm and loving toward him. The murder was committed a week later, and the father was arrested and tried for it. John was in terror during the trial that he would be called on to testify and have to say that his father was guilty. Later he repressed the entire incident and all during the rest of his life had consciously strongly believed the family myth that his father had been unjustly railroaded to a life sentence in prison because a rising young state attorney general wanted to make his own reputation so as to run for higher office.

In his early 40s, John developed a malignant melanoma that was completely resistant to treatment. Presently a metastasis appeared on the uvula that blocked his ability to eat or drink. Surgery was scheduled. The morning before the day of the surgery, during a psychotherapy session, he suddenly recalled the entire episode. With a tremendous outpouring of emotion he relived the scene and his subsequent childhood feelings. This went on for four hours, leaving both him and the psychotherapist exhausted. At the end of that time (two o'clock in the afternoon), he sank into a deep and apparently peaceful sleep (and I went back to my office to change my shirt!). That evening he was hungry and ate and managed to swallow some food without difficulty. The next afternoon the surgeon (Dr. Bernard Welt) came in to make a final check before the surgery. He observed such a marked change in the metastasis that he delayed the surgery until, as he wrote in the chart, "the meaning of this unprecedented change becomes apparent." Two days later the metastasis had completely disappeared and the surgery was canceled.

The catharsis here had a major specific effect. However, to the best of my ability to determine, it had no effect on his attitudes toward himself, his relationships with others, or with the cosmos at large. It also seemed to have no effect on the general development of the melanoma, and he died of it a few months later.

————•◆•————

Psychotherapy was originally a service profession. This has markedly changed in the past forty years, and it is now, for a very large percentage of the practitioners, a business activity. We can see one aspect of this change in the advertisements in the house organs of such organizations as the American Psychological Association and the American Psychiatric Association. In, for example, *The Psychological Monitor* of the Psychological Association, a large percentage of the ads concern billing practices and methods for keeping your practice full. Some of the methods advertised go into detail as to techniques for increasing your patient load and have not the slightest indicators of how this will help your patients or increase the percentage of positive results. (See Figure 4–1, for a fictionalized, yet typical ad of this sort.) Indeed, the "success" of a professional psychotherapy practice is generally calculated by its size rather than by how many of the patients in it are actually helped.

One way to gauge the attitude of a therapist, so far as this area goes, is to ask whether he or she has either a sliding scale of prices per session with the spread between the highest and lowest large enough to make a real difference or else contributes at least one half day a week to a free clinic. I personally will not refer to a therapist who does not fulfill one of these requirements. (A therapist who works more than thirty-odd hours a

Figure 4–1. *OVERFLOW*

Your Private Practice

* Bring addiction disorders into your office *in groups.*

* Have them remain for a twelve-week training program.

* Have those who require more treatment remain for further psychotherapy.

* Generate a waiting list to fill in seasonal dips.

This program will bring *financial security* to your private practice. For complete information, fill in and mail the tear sheet below.

— — — — — — — — — — — — — — — — — —

Please Send Me More Information

Name _____

Address _____

City/State Zip _____

Mail to:

Name of Counseling Center

Street

City

week is certainly one to avoid. No one can give their best if they have a heavier schedule than that.)

———•◆•———

Another way in which psychotherapists differ from each other is on how they view the question of why people come to the office and work with them. Some see the patients as primarily being driven to undertake this work in order to end or lessen a painful or distressing symptom. Others of us see this as perhaps a triggering factor but believe that there is, in human beings, a deep drive and desire to grow and become closer to their potential. Therapists who believe in this tend also to feel that it is the basic reason that most patients come to the office. This difference in the viewpoints of therapists essentially mirrors the belief of one group that human beings are essentially motivated by a homeostatic drive—a drive to reduce distressing stimuli—and the belief of the other that there is a strong human drive to potentiating the self, to, in Kurt Goldstein's term, self-actualize.

These generally unverbalized differences have profound effects on our behavior as therapists. An additional complication is that our view on this matter and that of a specific patient often differ and that this difference is never clarified. The confusions resulting from this may seriously impede the progress of therapy.

———•◆•———

Although most of us were trained that when we see a patient, we should establish a diagnosis, we should be clear that a diagnosis has only three purposes. The first is to have something to put down on paper in order to satisfy the accountants who determine third-party payments. For them the diagnosis should be something out of the latest accepted manual, probably one that was primarily designed for the purpose of keeping computer records. The *DSM* series is a good example of this.

The second purpose of a diagnosis is that it is sometimes useful in pointing out which, if any, of the mind-affecting drugs might be helpful. Since research is usually done in terms of the relationships between specific diagnoses and the effectiveness of individual drugs, we must generally operate in these terms. Once, however, you really get a feel for a specific drug and its effects or find someone who has this sense and sensitivity, you can largely forget about the diagnoses and prescribe in terms of this individual patient. However, people with this kind of sensitivity are rare (I have never met one, for example, among the physicians who call themselves "psychopharmacologists" and who generally know a lot about chemistry and amazingly little about human beings.)

The third reason for a diagnosis on a particular patient is to tell us how little we know about this person. We know so little that we can only see the similarities that they have to one defined group and not the differences—not what makes them the unique and special person they are.

If this idea seems too outrageous, I might point out that Bertrand Russell once said that the reason physics is mathematical is because we know so little about reality. "We know so little," said Russell, "that we can only determine reality's mathematical aspects." The same can be said of psychological diagnoses—they remind us that we know so little of this person that we are able to fit them into a classification. Once we do this, we are in great danger, if we have not already succumbed to it, of losing the human being in front of us.

To put this matter in clearer perspective, we might say that a diagnosis is useful for the aforementioned reasons and, as a part of the last reason, for helping us when we are beginning to know a patient. At that time a diagnosis of schizoid personality, for example, will help us know some of the limitations of the person in front of us. We know something about reasonable expectations, how strongly we can push or interpret, and so forth. Later as we get to know this person better, we *personalize* the diagnosis. Mr. Jones, with a specific diagnosis, and Ms. Robinson with the same *DSM-IV* (1994) number after her name, are two very different people. However, only as we get to know them and to be aware of their uniqueness will the images of them in our minds (and therefore our behavior toward them) differentiate. But *unless* we are aware that a formal diagnosis is largely a statement of ignorance, this will be much less likely to happen.

In terms of the need to satisfy the administrative and accountant types who control third-party payments (and insist on a formal diagnosis in the charts in clinics and hospitals), there is one *DSM-IV* number that I have found very useful. The number 309-28 (Adjustment Disorder with Mixed Emotional Features, p. 128) states that the person is neither "neurotic" nor "psychotic" nor yet a "character disorder" or anything else. It states that the person is a basically and formally "normal" individual who is having trouble facing the present vissicitudes and problems of life and needs help to get through them in the best possible and least painful way. This, of course, describes all of us except that the patient's problems are large enough to bring him to seek help and he has had the courage to do so. It is a diagnosis that cannot follow the patient and bring trouble to him in later life.

Interestingly enough, this diagnosis was devised by the United States Army in the early 1940s to describe men who did very well in civilian life but were not suited temperamentally to the army life. The treatment recommended was to give them an honorable discharge, which tended to solve the problems pretty quickly. Many of these who we examined and gave this diagnosis to in the army were individuals who would have been described as "healthy" by any psychologist or psychiatrist who examined them when they had been civilians or after they were returned to civilian life.

5

ON BEING
A THERAPIST

I have never forgotten an incident that occurred many years ago with my then supervisor, Marthe Gassmann. After we had worked together for a few months, one day she said to me, "Larry, isn't it about time we started getting you educated?" I replied that I thought a Ph.D. from the University of Chicago and five years' army experience as a psychologist meant something. Marthe answered, "Oh, yes, you are pretty knowledgeable about what is in the textbooks. You know nomenclature and diagnosis by their formal signs. You know the difference between a Freudian and Jungian approach and what is the latest research on schizophrenia. But the best minds of our race have been trying for a very long time to understand what it means to be human and in the human condition. And they did not write in psychology or psychiatry or social work journals. They wrote plays and poetry and novels; they composed music and painted pictures and sculpted statues. They did research in philosophy and history. And about these things, Larry, you are an ignoramus. You love poetry and that is a start. You are a pretty good mechanic in your work and are well on the way to becoming a better one. But you have to decide whether you want to be a mechanic or a therapist. Which is it?"

I sulked for awhile and allowed that I wanted to become a therapist. She smiled and said, "I hoped and thought you would say that. Here." She handed me a piece of paper she had obviously previously prepared. On it was a list of readings—some Plato, some Carlyle, *Paradise Lost*, and some others. Also some particular recordings of classical music to listen to and some pictures at the Metropolitan Museum of Art to see. When I had completed that list, she gave me others. After a period of time I went on my own and eventually found the particular approaches to the human condition that were most meaningful to me and that helped me see my patients in a wider and deeper context than the textbooks could. (They were Greek classic philosophy and nineteenth-century English poetry.)

Knowing what is in the textbooks is absolutely essential for a therapist. He or she *must* have read Freud, Jung, Adler, Angyal, Goldstein, Sullivan, Horney, and a variety of others. And must comprehend what these giants were about and saying. But they are not enough. In the logician's terms, they "are necessary, but not sufficient." They are true and valid, but they only encompass a small part of what it means to be human.

To this day, I will not refer a patient to a psychotherapist unless he or she has a deep knowledge of at least one other field of wisdom besides what is in our texts. This other field may be classical music or history or philosophy or art. One of the people I refer to comes from the best of the Yoga tradition and brings the comprehensions of that field to bear. One has a profound knowledge of art history. Another has a deep comprehension and love of classical music. Another was trained in philosophy, and so forth.

I might emphasize this concept by pointing out that if we want knowledge of the very special things that make us human, if we want comprehension of love, terror, religious awe, dignity, courage, or sacrifice, we do not go to the psychology or psychiatry textbooks, or to the Journal of this or that. We go to Tolstoy and Dostoyevsky, to Schubert and Mozart, to Goya and Rodin, to Browning, Millay, and Austen.

The amount of understanding and communication we can have of and with another person depends largely on how rich and broad a background we can bring to the relationship. When a patient speaks to us of his experience with murderous thoughts, our comprehension will be much more profound if we not only bring to the situation our own experience of our own murderous thoughts (and this is one reason, of course, that long and serious psychotherapy is *essential* if one wishes to be a psychotherapist—so we can bring our own experience to our work) but also have learned about this type of feeling from Iago, Clytemnestra, and Raskolnikov. If our patient speaks to us of loving, our comprehension is greater if we have learned not only from our own loving but also from Anna Karenina, Elizabeth Barrett Browning, and the Shakespeare sonnets.

A very wide training is important if we wish to be psychotherapists and "meet" and "comprehend" and "communicate with" other people. The more I know of human consciousness and behavior in its widespread forms, the more likely I am to comprehend a particular "other." If I have experienced Prince Mishkin through the genius of Dostoyevsky, I am more likely to *know* the experience of a particular patient who is striving to awaken himself to something he does not yet comprehend but knows is within his potential than if I had not read *The Idiot*. If I have been touched by Schubert's *Die Wintereise*, I am far more able to understand the sadness of another person's experience. If I have met and listened to Socrates through the love Plato had for him, I am more likely to be able to understand the New York City Ilyosha Karamazov who tells me that it is better to suffer injustice than it is to commit it.

As a seasoned telegrapher listens to the same staccato blur of sounds that I do and, in it, because of his training and experience, meets, and does not doubt that he meets, another human being and *hears* him, so the more training and experience I have, the more likely I am to meet and hear another person through the blur of signals he or she sends out.

In order to organize our knowledge and be able to use it as therapists, we must also have learned Freud, Sylvano Arieti, and Carl Rogers. This is essential but far from enough. The task of a therapist is constantly to grow himself, to expand his experience and his soul so that he not only can bring more and more to his patients but also can say to them, "Do as I do, as well as say." We teach, in the deepest way, by example. If a therapist wants his patients to grow, he must himself constantly struggle to grow. He must understand what Meister Eckhart meant in the fourteenth century when he wrote:

There is no stopping place in this world, no, nor was there ever one for any man, no matter how far along his path he'd come. This above all then, be always ready for the gifts of God and always for new ones. And always remember, God is a thousand times more ready to give than you are to receive!

To understand the meaning and *tone* of our patient's experience we need Shakespeare and Schubert, Picasso and Rilke. To understand the *structure* of these experiences and how the reactions to them can be modified, we need Freud and Jung, Otto Rank and Alfred Adler, Harry Stack Sullivan and Adolph Meyer, Karl Menninger and Victor Frankl.

The goal of training in psychology—what we really wish to teach our students—is to comprehend how character and personality develop, change, grow. How the themes and parts of an individual swell and recede and form harmonious and unharmonious patterns. How different patterns of being respond to different environmental patterns. In these areas we humans have learned much—Shakespeare knew more than Homer, and Arthur Miller knows things that Shakespeare did not (e.g., about the effect of culture on personality development). Yet there is much to learn, and we hope to progress in comprehension of what it means to be a human being. To do this, however, we must concentrate on the whole person, on the richness and complexity that makes us what we are and must take our orientation as much from Tolstoy as from Beck, Minuchin, or Lacan.

————•◆•————

We often associate a particular technique with a specific person and then go on to feel that it is their technique that accounts for their dramatic results. This is a false conclusion. Fritz Perls did not get such good results because he used Gestalt technique. He obtained the results because he was Fritz Perls, using a technique to help him relate as a person to another person. This is shown by the fact that nobody else gets the results he got when they use the Gestalt method. We can learn much from Perls's approach, but to *use* it routinely instead of when it really fits the pairing of the two of you, when it comes "trippingly off the tongue," is a clear violation of Miale's Law.

There is much for us to learn from Rogers's nondirective approach and from Felix Deutsche's Associative Amanneunsis and from Beck on interacting with families, but none of these are *the* correct or *the* right way. Psychotherapy is a relationship between humans, and this relationship must be human and therefore different in each case.

Irvin Yalom puts this very clearly in his *Existential Psychotherapy*:

> No, a therapist helps a patient not by sifting through the past but by being lovingly present with that person; by being trustworthy, interested; and by believing that their joint activity will ultimately be redemptive and healing. The drama of age regression and incest recapitulation (or, for that matter, any therapeutic cathartic or intellectual project) is healing only because it provides therapist and patient with some interesting shared activity while the real therapeutic force—the relationship—is ripening on the tree. [quoted in Willis 1994, p. 116]

———◆———

Psychotherapy developed in the early part of this century when the prestige of nineteenth-century physics was at its height. ("The physics of one generation is the metaphysics of the next," wrote Max Planck.) It was widely believed that physics before 1900 had developed *the* ultimate scientific method, and the only thing remaining was to apply it in new areas and to new questions. One of the central tenets of this scientific method was the concept that science should be value-free. Only the facts were important; the scientific researcher should never let beliefs or moral values interfere with the perception and understanding of the facts.

There are, however, fields of science that have made real progress in which this concept is not accepted as true.

In ethology it has been found that, in Konrad Lorenz's words, you must "love" the animal you are working with:

> It takes a very long period of watching to become really familiar with an animal and to attain a deeper understanding of its behavior; and without the love for the animal itself, no observer however patient could ever look at it long enough to make valuable observations on its behavior. [quoted in Lehner 1979, p. 11]

As another leading ethologist, Frank Darling, put it, you must be "intimate" with your subject. Imagine sending to a typical journal (*The American Journal of Psychotherapy* and *Orthopsychiatry* come to mind) an article that included a statement that you "loved" your subjects or were "intimate" with them. The article would bounce so fast it would not even be marked "Rejected. The Editor." Rather, it would come back stamped "Opened by Mistake! The Editor."

———— • ◆ • ————

In history today there is the basic concept that to understand what a particular period was all about, a mere compilation of the facts is not enough—not the facts of dates and battles and decisions. Instead, we must, in Robin Collingwood's (1940) words, "Think their thoughts, feel their feelings" (p. 27). Caesar was killed at the door of the Senate house. We know where and when. But if we are modern historians we also need to feel what Brutus and Cassius felt, to understand what they thought they were doing. Only then can we understand. To quote Collingwood:

> To the historian, the activities whose history he is studying are not spectacles to be watched, but experiences to be lived through in his own mind. They are objective, or known to him, only because they are also subjective, or activities of his own. [p. 29]

And if we wish to comprehend the actions of a child, we must, as Eda LeShan, a noted professional colleague of mine, has so cogently pointed out, remember the child within ourselves. Those who do not remember themselves as children in a similar situation cannot really comprehend how a child feels. We have certainly learned this in psychotherapy. Only with the empathy that comes from self-understanding and self-exploration can we comprehend our clients. (This, by the by, is one of the reasons that therapists' having had a long, serious period of psychotherapy themselves is one of the criteria by means of which we distinguish the psychotherapists from the charlatans.)

Further, our experience in psychotherapy has taught us that maintaining an *objective* attitude is not conducive to the patient's progress. We must *care* about the patient; we must be deeply and emotionally concerned about the best for him. For positive results to be likely. The new definition of *countertransference* (originally given by Rollo May) is that it is "the ability to *enthusiastically* affirm the patient's growth and development."

In those areas of the study of consciousness and behavior in which we have made real progress in understanding and helping our strange and suffering species

—psychotherapy, history, child development, ethology —we have found that we cannot progress without empathy, love, and personal involvement with our subject. (These, of course, are not enough by themselves. Training, long and hard, and discipline are also needed.)

A basic tenet of psychotherapy has long been that moral values have no place in the process; nothing is morally "right" or morally "wrong." But the idea of "no judgmentalism" is equated with that of "no ethical values," and few recognize that this is in itself a value system. As Rollo May (1953) put it, "A lack of value judgments which the older therapy opted for is based on a definite philosophical system—that of a fairly complete relativism" (p. 364).

In his usual succinct manner, Gardner Murphy (1958), universally recognized in the profession as one of our most valuable and outstanding psychologists, has summed up both the older approach and his view of it:

> The dogmatic rationalism first uttered by Thomas Huxley, later echoed by Bertrand Russell, announced that for an enlightened, modern person, ethics is clearly a local artifact of special conditions of society, and that man can count on no cosmic support whatever for any ethical goals with which he wishes to concern himself. These confident expressions are all interesting, if quaint, responses to the empirical and practical difficulties of determining where we are, where we are going, and what we are. [p. 176]

If psychotherapists have begun to realize everything is judged to be relative (to the culture, to the social class, to the family, and so on), then therapists are saying, in effect, "If you want a system of behavior, look around you and take the most convenient—that is, the most common." If value judgments are not openly made by therapists, the patient is likely to accept the superficial mores of his culture.

It is, of course, not possible to keep ethical values completely out of therapy. As the psychiatrist Thomas Szasz (1958) says:

> [I]t does make a difference—arguments to the contrary notwithstanding—what the psychiatrists' socioethical orientations happen to be, for these will influence his ideas on what is wrong with the patient, what deserves comment or interpretation, in what possible directions change might be possible, and so forth. . . . Can anyone really believe that a psychotherapist's ideas concerning religious beliefs, slavery, or other similar issues, play no role in his practical work? [p. 115]

While it is not possible to keep values out of therapy, it has been possible to try to convince the patient that the therapy was "above" values or ethical judgments. "An amoral psychotherapy," as psychologist Goodwin Watson (1958) pointed out in a classic paper, "is a contradiction in terms" (p. 575).

Psychologist George Turner (1960), discussing this relativity of values, indicates that because the Freudian superego is culturally defined and limited, it does not necessarily follow that all values are: "Without challenging the reality of the Freudian conscience, one can deny it exclusive rights to the territory" (p. 155). As a possible example, he gives the existentialist concept of *ontological* guilt, an apparently culture-free form of guilt that arises from forfeiting one's potentialities.

Rollo May (1953), after suggesting a redefinition of objectivity for the therapist ("Objectivity is the capacity to affirm the growth and development of the other person" [p. 350]), gives some examples of value judgments possible in therapy. These include the concept that it is better for a human being to have the ability to use his capacities and potentials, to be free and to love, than it is for him not to do these things. Further, that in interpersonal relationships, one should so act as to encourage and aid these developments in others.

A general movement toward the acceptance of values in therapy is now in progress. There is a growing feeling that being "free" of moral judgments leads to loss of self-respect, identity, and self-image. Acceptance of the idea that all the patient's undesirable behavior is due to the sins of the parents appears to weaken concepts of will, responsibility, and self-control. A *New Yorker* cartoon showed two juvenile delinquents awaiting their appearance in court. The older one is advising the younger, "You can get off easy. Just tell them that your mother hated you."

This perhaps brings up another reason for the open acceptance of ethical values in therapy. Only then is it possible for the patient to distinguish between neurotic guilt and real guilt and to understand that these two must be responded to very differently. We analyze neurotic guilt and get rid of it by understanding its source. With real guilt we resolve to learn from what we did and never do it again. Then we make restitution—to the person or persons harmed, if possible. If it is not possible to do this, we make restitution to others in need.

To repeat, in the development of therapy the early pioneers were concerned with being scientific as they understood the term. Therefore, they included the concept that the therapist should be value free and simply let the facts of the patient's life and existence come to consciousness and be verbalized. The theory was that this would somehow lead to curing the patient's problems since once they were conscious and he was no longer driven by unconscious forces, the problems and memories could be dealt with intellectually. What had been unconscious should now be at ego levels and could be handled with the help of the intellect. Therapy was, said Freud, "like the draining of the Zuyder Zee."

This may or may not have been a valid concept and a good idea. It was, however, impossible. There is no such thing as a value-free psychotherapy. It is an oxymoron, a contradiction in terms. Every psychoanalytic (or any other kind) of interpretation contains a tremendous number of assumptions, preconceptions, and a complete view of what reality "really" is. This is what the philosopher Edmund Husserl called "the enormous a priori." Even if one follows the strict rules of orthodox nondirective therapy, one still directs the process. For example, if the patient says three things in a sentence or paragraph and the therapist responds to one of them with an "um-hum," the very fact of the selection of the one is a directing of the process. Indeed, the organization of the therapist's office, the uniform he or she wears (as prescribed by the local subculture to which the therapist belongs), the type of greeting, payment arrangements, and just about everything else that goes on contains a good many hints, suggestions, and statements about reality and how to function within it. About all the therapist can do is to be clear about these matters and not be fooling himself that he is nondirective. Within this limit, the therapist can also be clear that there are a wide variety of lifestyles possible within this definition and try hard to help the patient find the courage to move in the direction of the lifestyle, the ways of being, relating, creating, that most fit him as a unique individual and that will bring the most real and long-lasting satisfaction and joy in life. As long as this life does not harm others and prevent them finding and moving toward *their* ideal lifestyle, the therapist can and should encourage it with a full heart. "Happiness," wrote Robert Heinlein, "is being allowed to work very hard for long hours for something you believe in." Helping the patients find and move toward working whatever is their natural goal is a central part of this work.

The idea that enthusiasm and zest are integral parts of health is also very much a part of the Western tradition of spiritual development. *The Cloud of Unknowing,* one of the most important medieval manuscripts on spirituality, strongly urges that the search for a relationship with God be "listy," the opposite of listless, passive, unenthusiastic. The writings of the Hassidic tradition are also filled with comments to the effect that true spiritual development must be "listy" and zestful. One should, say these writings, live with "fervor."

There is a classic story about St. Theresa of Avila. At one time she was the guest at a monastery. In honor of their famous visitor, the Abbott served a dish of roast partridges instead of the usual gruel for supper. St. Theresa tore into the dish with great and obvious enjoyment and gusto. The Abbott was horrified and reproved her with the words that it would be more seemly for a Bride of Christ to save such enthusiasm for her prayer. She replied, "Abbott, when its prayer time *pray*, and when its partridge time, *partridge!*"

To be a psychotherapist who is not enjoying his own life, who does not have a good deal of zest and enthusiasm for his daily existence, is a strange concept indeed. Surely anyone who is embroiled in life has hard and difficult times, but apart from these inevitabilities, anyone who is a therapist should be first of all a person who is working on his own path in a way and at a pace that provides excitement and joy. Otherwise, what message is one giving one's patients? Who would go to a gymnasium instructor with a soft and flabby body? And yet, unless our own life reflects the kind of goal in life that we are trying to help our patients achieve, that is a good metaphor for the state of affairs.

If the therapist is not showing in his or her life patterns and style a fierce and tender concern for all of him- or herself, how can he or she hope to help the patient to achieve this? And if there is no laughter and joy on the path, why work on it? "God save me from sober and serious saints!" said Theresa of Avila, and we might well say the same thing about psychotherapists.

———◆———

In this book I have been concerned with what we have learned about gardening each other with this new technique of ours called psychotherapy. This approach to helping one individual at a time, or a small group at a time, is one of the greatest human advances we have ever made. I have devoted a large portion of my adult life to learning a little about it and do not regret any of this expenditure of time and energy.

But it is far from enough. If certain present trends (with which we are all familiar) continue, our species is doomed to extinction, and all our actions and efforts will have no meaning. These trends include the ever increasing size of the population and the cutting off of our oxygen supply through the poisoning of the oceans and the destruction of the rain forests. Unless we recognize, and vigorously act on the recognition, that we are a part of and involved in the human race and that our race is under mortal threat, our work and our knowledge are useless. There *are* organizations fighting to maintain a planet on which we can live. Unless we, at the very least, give them our enthusiastic support, our efforts, as psychotherapists and as human beings, are a sham and hypocrisy. For the sake of our species, we must remember the deep truth Adlai Stevenson (1965) was expressing when he wrote:

> We all travel together, passengers on a little spaceship, dependent on its vulnerable supplies of air and soil, all committed for our safety to its security and peace, preserved from annihilation only by the care, the work, and I will say the love we give our fragile craft. [p. 17]

As we move into the twenty-first century after a hundred years of experience at our craft, as we reassert our old traditions and become oriented to heal as well as to cure, as we integrate what we have learned into what we are doing, these words of Adlai Stevenson must point to a major aspect of our behavior, both as individual human beings and as psychotherapists.

Appendix I

A LARGE-SCALE EXPERIMENT ON THE BASIC NATURE OF HUMAN BEINGS

Generally speaking, psychologists tend to hold one of three views about the basic nature of humankind: the view of Hobbes and Freud that humans are basically hostile and narcissistic, the view of the French Encyclopedists and the Behaviorists that there is no such thing as a basic nature, and the view of Rousseau and Rogers that they are basically sociable and forward looking. Ten pairs of groups of 250 S's each (N = 5,000) were exposed to each other under experimental conditions. Results strongly favor the Rousseau-Rogers viewpoint.

In 1953, Carl Rogers wrote:

> One of the most revolutionary concepts to grow out of our clinical experience is the growing recognition that the innermost core of man's nature, the deepest levels

of his personality, the base of his "animal nature" is positive in character—is basically socialized, forward-moving, rational and realistic. [p. 184]

This is a very clear statement of a viewpoint, but it has not, to my knowledge, been anywhere subjected to experimental test. It is, therefore, a statement of faith, not of science.

Those who hold the opposite view—that the "basic nature" of humankind is that of a self-oriented carnivore who must be tamed and trained by society—also are depending on faith rather than on science. Among others, those with a psychoanalytic orientation follow this view. They, of course, frequently are not aware that the basic orientation of psychoanalysis is in this direction and that the techniques only make sense in terms of it.

Similarly, the individuals who identify themselves as "humanistic" psychologists and psychiatrists are frequently not aware of the basic orientation in this viewpoint and that its techniques only make sense in terms of this orientation. This is an age in which the "scientist," "professional," and "layman" tend to ignore and depreciate metaphysics. This has led to a large number of individuals being unaware of their own metaphysics and has slowed scientific understanding considerably. It has led to such disasters as that frequently seen in "group therapy." A technique devised—and only making sense—within a "humanistic" metaphysics was adopted by many with a "psychoanalytic" metaphysics. Since in this second view the basic nature of people is hostile and narcissistic, we saw many therapeutic groups completely oriented to "getting out the hostility" in which the belief of the group and leader frequently is that only negative drives are "authentic," "real," and basic" and that all expressions of warmth, caring, altruism, and so on, are evasions. With this basic belief system, the underlying idea of group therapy— to permit fuller expression of the deeper feelings— hardly makes much sense.

Although the problem of the basic nature of a human being has been largely ignored, it will not go away. One group of psychologists has solved it by deciding that it does not exist, that there is no such thing as a basic nature, but everything depends on cultural training. These are believers in a compete *tabula rasa*, one so blank that it does not, in their view, respond more easily to one type of experience than another.

The problem is a very old one. In ancient China Mencius believed that humankind is innately good, Hsun Tzu that it is innately evil. Hobbes believed that humankind in the "natural state" was "nasty, brutish, short-lived and cold"; Rousseau that he was a "noble savage." Sartre advanced the viewpoint that we have no essential nature at all.

We have today in psychology three basic groups (with a variety of schismatic subgroups), each with its own approach to the basic nature of a human being. First there are those who follow the lines of Hsun Tzu, Hobbes, and Freud. Human beings, in their natural state, are hostile and feral predators concerned only with the satisfaction of their own wishes. Society tames and trains the beasts and teaches them to behave in a socially acceptable manner. The second group, following the lines of the French Encyclopedists, Sartre, and the Behaviorists, believes that there is no basic nature at all and that essentially all behavior is the result of experience. The wide divergence of behavior among individuals is seen as due to differences in conditioning, reinforcement, and training. The third group follows the line of Mencius, Rousseau, Maslow, and Rogers. Humankind in the "natural state" is noble and loving. These basically positive characteristics of feeling and behaving are warped, deformed, and often buried completely by the individual's society and upbringing.

It is clear that whichever view one holds (whether or not this is done with conscious awareness), it will strongly influence one's view of oneself and others, one's behavior as patient or psychotherapist, as well as what published material in the social sciences you read or skip, consider to be valid or to be nonsense.

Adherence to one or another of these camps has been based on personal experience, one's interpretation of it, and faith. On this crucial issue there has been remarkably little direct experimentation. The experiment of mine that follows is an attempt to begin to fill that gap.

Method

Twenty groups of individuals (N of each group greater than 250) are to be divided at random into ten pairs of two groups each. The members of each pair will be briefly presented to each other under the following conditions:

1. They would be able to see each other but not physically touch each other.
2. The groups would have never seen each other before and would be reasonably certain that they would never see each other again.
3. The groups would be selected from a variety of different countries so as to minimize national and cultural characteristics. These would include such differences as communist and noncommunist, countries

between which there is good feeling, and countries between which there is tension.

4. Members of all groups would be free from special pressures such as hunger, thirst, economic threat, and so on. They would not be in a physical situation that would build up frustrations (and thereby *possibly* build up the probability of aggressive responses).

5. Each group would be randomly divided into at least three subgroups for the purpose of the experiment. The subgroups would be out of visual range of each other during the encounter with the other members of the pair. The purpose of this would be to prevent one charismatic member from setting off a chain reaction in any group. At most, such an individual, if present, could only affect one subgroup during the encounter.

Thus, we have a situation in which large groups of people, from a variety of backgrounds, briefly encounter each other in a completely safe, nonthreatening environment and will never meet with each other again. They can respond in perfect safety in any way they wish. They can shout epithets, shake their fists, or otherwise express hostility. They can behave individualistically or in subgroups with no consistent pattern. They can behave consistently in a warm and friendly fashion, expressing positive affect. The experiment is so designed that they have nothing to gain or lose by any of these behaviors so that they can respond according to their "basic natures." The N of over 5,000 persons, divided into 20 groups and 60 subgroups, and coming from at least 10 different countries, should minimize individual variations and special cultural fashions.

Twenty groups were selected, each with an N of 250 or over. Each was divided into three or more subgroups.

Ten pairs were assigned at random. The two groups in each dyad viewed each other at between 50 and 100 yards for approximately one minute each. All participants were reasonably certain that they would never meet members of the other group again or, if this somehow happened, that they would not be able to identify each other as coparticipants in the experiment. Selected groups came from Italy, France, Norway, Russia, Greece, Turkey, Romania, Yugoslavia, West Germany, England, and the United States.

The Null Hypothesis was that the Hobbes–Freud hypothesis as to the basic nature of human beings is correct and that, under these conditions, the subjects would consistently express hostility toward each other by means of gesture and epithet.

The Null Hypothesis would be disproven in two ways. Individuals or subgroups could behave in random fashion (so far as the warmth–hositility parameter is concerned). This would indicate in favor of the *tabula rasa* theory. If there was a consistent expression of warm and friendly emotion, this would indicate in favor of the Rousseau-Maslow-Rogers theory.

Results

The experiment was done on August 20, 1978, at the entrance to the Grand Canal in Venice. The groups were passengers on cruise liners entering or leaving the harbor. Ships entering and leaving passed each other slowly at between 50 and 100 yards, with approximately one minute of clear viewing time of each other by the passengers gathered at the rail. The passengers on each liner were on at least three separate decks and thus effectively divided into subgroups. Passengers on each ship gathered at the rail facing the other liner numbered by eye inspection–over 250.

The subgroups were completely consistent in their behavior. All sixty or more subgroups of all ten pairs behaved actively in a warm, friendly fashion toward the groups on the ship facing them. There was a great deal of waving and smiling. In the more than 5,000 individuals observed in this experiment, there was not one single hostile or derogatory expression or feeling noted. The intensity of the positive gestures varied widely, with a sizable minority of the S's ignoring the passing liner or gazing at it with no discernable emotion expressed However, all expressions observed—and these were made by a large majority of the S's—were of a positive nature. The Null Hypothesis is disproved, and the experiment indicates strongly in favor of the Rousseau-Maslow-Rogers hypothesis.

Discussion

The purpose of this paper is to dramatize the importance of research in a much neglected area of psychology today. This area—the basic nature of humankind—is one on which there are very strong opinions and on which entire systems of psychotherapy are based. The fact that these opinions are rarely verbalized and that the dependence of most therapeutic methods on a hypothesis concerning the matter is little understood makes matters worse. We respond to things as we believe they are and treat ourselves and others according to what we believe human beings are. This is the most elementary common sense, but most of us—including most professionals in psychology—have not explored or verbalized our beliefs. It may well be that if we did, some of us might change our basic beliefs, and perhaps then change some of our therapeutic methods and other behaviors.

In spite of the rather pompous academese in which this report of a set of observations is couched, I would not care to have to defend its scientific methodology and its conclusions. Nevertheless, there is something there. In the words made immortal by the last line of 10,000 Ph.D. theses: "Further research is needed in this area."

Appendix II

MODELS AND METAPHORS FOR BEING HUMAN

An idea that psychology took from the physical sciences as a basic concept was that you can—and for real understanding you *must*—make a model, a metaphor, for anything you are studying. Any entity, or class of occurrences, can be better understood as a metaphor and then can be studied and researched as such. In part, this came from the experience of Descartes and others that much of the action of mechanical objects could be best understood through examining graphs, charts, and tables of mathematical formulas. If, for example, as Descartes found, you wished to teach artillery men how to charge and elevate their cannons so as to hit a specific target, you gave them mathematical tables to use. They did much better looking at these than they did looking at the target.

This concept—that scientific understanding of an entity, event, or process is increased by making a model of it and then manipulating the model—is both subtle and profound. It has been seen all through the scientific field since the seventeenth century. An atom is modeled as a miniature solar system. An electron is modeled as a wave or a particle. The evolution of a species is visualized as a tree with dividing branches. The development of a civilization is modeled on the seasons of the year. To a Marxist, the evolution of society is that of a machine, inexorably developing on lines as predetermined as those of a clock.

This concept has been of great value in the field of molar physics and of mechanics generally. Here the mechanical model was applied and, once it was understood, accurately described the phenomena we were dealing with. The tremendous success of physics and mechanics in the nineteenth century was largely fostered by the use of the mechanical model *in the fields in which it was valid.*

In the human sciences, however, it is a different matter. Here the use of models has had an entirely opposite effect. Any model we have used for human beings has slowed and impeded our progress. The technique, so useful in physics, has not been applicable to our work.

One psychologist, Albert Chapanis (1966), put it:

Like Descartes, modellists seem to be inspired by the latest physical theories and playthings. Newton's mechanics brought forth models of man which treated him simply as a machine made up of levers and similar linkages. Watt's steam engine and the development of thermodynamics produced models of man which viewed him as nothing but a complicated heat engine. When servo-mechanisms mushroomed during World War II, we heard that man is nothing but a servo system. Somewhat more recently communication theory has been translated into models which purport to show that man is only an information handling system. [p. 105]

A recent quotation in the journal *Advances* said this another way:

Caveat Emptor: The Brain Is Not a Piece of Technology

Because we don't understand the brain very well we're constantly tempted to use the latest technology as a model for trying to understand it.

In my childhood we were always assured that the brain was a telephone switchboard ("What else could it be?"). And I was amused to see that Sherrington, the great British neuroscientist, thought that the brain worked like a telegraph system. Freud often compared the brain to hydraulic and electro-magnetic systems. Leibniz compared it to a mill, and now, obviously, the metaphor is the digital computer. . . .

The computer is probably no better and no worse as a metaphor for the brain than earlier mechanical metaphors. We learn as much about the brain by saying it's a computer as we do by saying it's a telephone switchboard, a telegraph system, a water pump, or a steam engine. [Searle 1984, p. 4]

The simplicity of the various images of human beings that have been used by psychologists, and the fact that they have very little (or nothing) to do with human experience, demonstrate how psychologists have been looking for human beings everywhere except where they are. There is the old teaching story of the Sufis concerning the man who spent the night searching on the ground under a lamppost. When a friend asked him what he was doing, he said that he was searching for the keys to his house. After helping him search for some time, the friend asked him if he was certain he had lost them under the lamppost. "Oh, no," said the man, "I lost them at home, but there is more light here."

There is only *apparently* more light where the psychologists have been searching for man. And he is not likely to be found in the same place the physical sciences find what they are looking for. Meister Eckhart once said that if you are searching for God, you should look in the place you lost Him. We might legitimately paraphrase this by saying that if you are searching for man, look where you lost him. Or, at least, in the natural environments where he is to be found.

Models only work for the simplest and most trivial aspects of human activity and consciousness. Given anything more meaningful and more important than the extinction of a conditioned eye blink, they stop working. We, as a science, have refused to accept that the correct model of a human being is a human being. There is no reason not to be anthropomorphic when we are studying anthropos. You, I, Iago, and Mr. George Babbitt are not rats, computers, or the hyphen between a stimulus and a response, and to try to explain us as such is to look at an outmoded theory of science, not the data of our field.

A computer is a brain to the same degree that the Palomar telescope is an eye or a bulldozer is a muscle, or vice versa.

It is interesting to note that every scientist who advocates a particular model leaves out one human being as an exception. Each says, "All humans behave as they do because they are a rat or a telephone exchange or a computer. But I write this book or give this lecture for entirely different reasons—I do it because I am a human being with intelligence and free will and altruistic motives."

And, of course, they must do this for two reasons. First, their *experience* tells them that they are not a hyphen between a stimulus and response operating purely because of conditioning chains. Second, because if they did not offer themselves as exceptions, who would pay any attention to them? If a B. F. Skinner wrote that his book said what it said because of his early or recent conditioning, why should we buy the book or pay any attention to it? After all, if he had been differently conditioned, we reason, he would have written something different.

Men love their wives, a speaker will state, because of cultural training, Oedipal displacement, or because they were accidentally conditioned to some of their wife's characteristics and therefore emit loving behavior. "I, however," this speaker will imply, "love my wife because she is so lovable." Again, the speaker has two reasons for his qualification. First, this is his actual experience. Second, he wants to be able to go home after the speech.

No historian, philosopher, or psychologist ever described his own research as due to a certain aspect of the class struggle, the need of his culture to dispose of excess productivity, or an inferiority complex. It is only the behavior of *others* that is determined by these motives. (It is easy to be reminded here of the psychoanalyst who, sitting in front of a wall of books, assures his patient that no one ever learned anything of importance, anything that changed his behavior to any significant degree, from books. Or of the French existentialist philosopher, writing book after book all with the same theme—that human beings cannot communicate with each other.)

The strange thing about all this is what we accept as reasonable in the mouths of psychologists talking about nonpsychologists we would consider psychotic in the mouths of nonpsychologists talking about themselves. And—to carry this very peculiar behavior on our part one step further—we accept as reasonable and worthy of consideration a psychologist saying certain things about others but would consider it very pathological behavior if he said the same things about himself.

To illustrate this, let us suppose a Behavioristic psychologist has written many papers proving that human beings have no free will and are controlled by their early and late conditioning. Now let us suppose that this person said, in ordinary conversation, that he himself was a machine, controlled by forces and events that he was often not consciously aware of, and that he had no choice over what he said or how he said it. And further, let us suppose he said that he was a machine talking to other machines (by which he meant his audience) and that none of these machines had any control over their behavior, but all were controlled by these accidental and random forces.

We would certainly consider this person seriously deranged. However, if he only discussed all other human beings who were not in the room and described them in these terms, we might consider him a legitimate scientist.

One wonders who "emits" the stranger and sicker behavior—the Behavioristic psychologists or those who take them seriously.

———◆·———

Each time we invent a new model or an old one again becomes chic, we are tempted (and generally give in to the temptation) to use it as a total explanatory system. The reflex, the birth order, the brain-as-computer, the mind-as-hydraulic-pump, the complex, the body type, the exact time and place of birth, the drive to self-realization, the human-as-white-rat, from time to time—all seem to serve us as ways to explain everything about human consciousness and behavior. Human beings tend to be as provincial in time as they are in space. And each time we do this, we do violence to the state of being human and to the person we are describing. I can discuss Oedipus, Richard the Lionheart, Robert E. Lee, Baron Richthofen, and Abraham Lincoln in any of these terms. However, when I am finished all I have is a flat two-dimensional picture. The *person* is lost.

We have developed what psychologist Gordon Allport describes as a "contempt for the psychic surface of life." There is always for us a deeper and hidden meaning. Isaiah Berlin (1981), the philosopher and economist, wrote of:

> the schools of thought which look upon human activity as being largely caused by occult and inescapable forces of which explicit social beliefs and theories are rationalizations—disguises to be penetrated and exposed. This is the heritage of marxism, of depth psychology, of the sociology of Pareto or Simmel or Mannheim. [p. 13]

In Joe Miller's *Joke Book*, an eighteenth-century collection of jokes, old when printed, is "Why does a chicken cross the road?" The answer, of course, is "To get to the other side." Think, however, of the answer the Behaviorist psychologist would give to the question! Or other learning theorists, or the Marxist, or the astrologer, or the depth psychologist. And if these answers are given to the chicken, then what about Columbus and the Atlantic?

The basic fact is that models make good tools but poor masters. I can view Columbus as the blind tool of a capitalist system that needed more raw materials and therefore extruded explorers from the central land mass of Europe. I can view him as driven by a compensation for an inferiority complex related to his family and his sibling position. I can see his behavior as impelled by the fact he was a male Gemini (or whatever sign he was born under). But if I wish to comprehend Christopher Columbus and why he persevered in the face of overwhelming discouragement and pain, then I must not lose the man in frames of reference that apply only to small parts of him. I must feel his feelings, see his vision, dream his dreams. I must conceptualize him as a human being like myself, not as a computer delivering its programming or a pigeon acting out its conditioning: Nor as a large upright rat, a servomechanism, a hologram, a telephone switchboard, or a flowering plant.

When Shylock finishes his great speech ("If you prick us, do we not bleed?"), we know him for another human being, and we comprehend a little more what that means and what human beings can feel, suffer, and do. We do not, at that moment, view him as a mechanism acting blindly and automatically in the grip of an Adlerian drive-to-power, a Freudian reaction-formation-to-passive-drivers, an Existentialist struggle-for-meaning, a Humanist will-to-become, or a Behaviorist machine responding to conditioning. And *this is* the reason that *The Merchant of Venice* contains more real psychology than shelf after shelf of psychology textbooks.

Another aspect of this difficulty with a model of a human being is that once we have one, we design our research on the basis of it. And thereby reinforce it. If I see man as a large, upright white rat, I will design studies that deal with ratlike characteristics, and the result of these studies will be that research shows man having ratlike characteristics, and so on.

If, however, I go in the opposite direction and use a model of man as a loving and altruistic goal seeker (until unfortunate socializing and educational experiences tie him up in knots and make him act in hostile ways) and see him as a sort of Ferdinand the Bull who *really* only wants to smell the flowers, then I will design experiments that show these characteristics and reinforce my own views. I will miss completely the complexity and the dark side of humanity. In both of these cases—and in all other models—we leave out a large part of the human being. The only model for anthropos is anthropos.

No experienced nursery school teacher, or other early-childhood educator working closely with children in a natural setting, believes that there is one model that, used properly, will "explain" all children. He or she will know that many models are necessary if you wish to use a model at all. The only useful model for a child, you will be told if you ask, *is* a child.

Similarly, the more experienced an ethologist is, the less use he or she will have for a concept of animals as entities whose behavior is determined by rigid, controlling instincts. The instinct model of animals breaks down when they are sufficiently observed in natural settings. If you want to know how children feel and behave, by and large do not go to a teacher of child psychology—go to a nursery school teacher. If you want to know how animals behave, do not by and large go to an animal psychologist—go to an ethologist.

In Voltaire's words, "History is only a pack of tricks we play on the dead." It is important to step back sometimes and ask ourselves whether the way psychotherapists describe their patients, fitting them into models whether or not they belong there, seeing them only through the eyes and lenses of a particular metaphor, is not a pack of tricks they play on the living. We can do the dead no harm.

And it is not that psychologists have not been repeatedly warned of the dangers and uselessness of making models of human beings and then explaining everything in terms of these models. As J. M. Cattell said in an 1895 presidential address to the American Psychological Association:

> We are past the time for simple explanations and systems, for metaphysics which explain everything in one way. The physiologist Ludwig in the 1880s wrote a classic textbook *Physiology* which explained everything on one basis—mechanism. Later he was asked why he did not prepare a new edition of it. He said, "Such a work must be written by a young man; an old man is too well aware of his ignorance. [p. 53]

Gordon Allport (1940), one of the few modern psychologists who comprehended that psychology needed a method of science adapted to human beings, wrote:

> A colleague . . . recently challenged me to name a single psychological problem not referable to rats for its solution. Considerably startled, I murmured something, I think, about the psychology of reading disability. But to my mind came flooding the historic problems of the aesthetic, humorous, religious, and cultural behavior of men. I thought how men build clavichords and cathedrals, how they write books, and how they laugh uproariously at Mickey Mouse; how they plan their lives five, ten or twenty years ahead; how, by an elaborate metaphysics of their own contrivance, they deny the utility of their own experience. . . . I thought of poetry and puns, of propaganda and revolution, of stock markets and suicide, and of man's despairing hopes. And of the elementary fact that human problem-solving,

unlike that of the rat, is saturated through and through with verbal function, so that we have no way of knowing whether the delay, the volition, the symbolizing and categorizing typical of human learning are even faintly adumbrated by findings in animal learning. [p. 14]

One anthropologist, A. D. W. Malefist (1974), put it:

Skinner has appropriately selected his subjects from pigeons and rats who can make only direct responses to stimuli. In order for man to be conditioned and manipulated in similar ways, it would be necessary to reduce him to a status similar to those captive animals and reduce him to the precultural, presymbolic and precreative level of existence, [p. 344]

From the anthropologist's viewpoint, animals and humans learn and respond in very different *kinds of ways*. Animals do not have symbolic speech and can only learn from immediate experience. No animal could conceive of a concept such as "We are of such stuff/As dreams are made on . . ." or "Glory be to God for dappled things." In the words of the philosopher and semanticist Alfred Korzybski (1951), "When a symbolic class of life enters the arena, hold your hats. All bets are off."

The influence of unverbalized concepts from the sourcebook of nineteenth-century physics was so strong that we persisted despite such warnings. After all, consider how successful the physicists were with their model of the atom as a small solar system and the electron as a particle or a wave. We ignore the fact that every modern physicist knows that an atom does not function as a small solar system and that an electron is neither a particle nor a wave. (An electron is a set of numbers, and *any model that uses characteristics from the worlds of sense is wrong and makes advances in under-*

standing more difficult.) Unspoken assumptions are
stronger than spoken ones and are not changed by advances in understanding.

The influence of the model we use on our concept-
ualizations and on the way we think about and solve
problems is difficult to overestimate. Think of the gorgeous arrogance of writing a book titled *The Behavior
of Organisms*, whose title encompasses every animal
from protozoa to humans, after studying rats in highly
artificial situations for ten years. Then, after fifteen
more years of experiments, this time covering pigeons
as well as rats, writing a book called *Science and Human
Behavior*. This is indeed the "All animals are equal"
dogma with a vengeance. To B. F. Skinner, man is
merely a rat or pigeon *writ large*. He used experiments
with these animals to deal with such human activities
as utopia planning, education for social reform, and
understanding superstition. The mind boggles at this—
or would if there were such a thing as mind. (And do
you doubt that *yours* exists?)

Very few rats or pigeons have learned to march in
military formations, establish and cheat on income
taxes, or any other of the common behaviors of the
human race. Nor have they learned to establish a Red
Cross for disaster relief, to compose the Fifth Symphony, or to paint *Christina's World*.

When the American psychologist went hunting animal behavior, he found one animal—the albino rat. It
was a boojum—the psychologist vanished softly and
suddenly away. In the two major journals, *The Journal
of Animal Behavior* and *The Journal of Comparative and
Physiological Behavior*, the more articles that were published, the fewer species they covered (Beach 1965). As
we published more and more in this field, it was literally about less and less. The end of the story is well

known. Edwin Chase Tolman dedicated his book *Purposive Behavior in Animals and Man* to the white rat. It has been the rat who has become the Pied Piper, leading the psychologists away from their homes, away from their concern with meaningful aspects of human life (Beach 1965).

In 1950 the psychologist Frank Beach (1965) surveyed the prestigious *Journal of Comparative and Physiological Psychology* and its forebears back to 1911. He concluded that a rather stable pattern had emerged and that psychology, as represented in this journal, had become the science of rat learning. A survey of this journal by psychologist Charles Kutscher (1971) showed that the rat, representing less than 0.001 percent of all living creatures, was used in 58 percent of reported studies. The rest of the studies used primates (11 percent), cats (5.1 percent), humans (9 percent), and birds (5 percent). Other species reports were less than 1 percent each.

The essential reasoning behind the use of rats and pigeons is that since all behavior consists of reflexes and since one reflex is very like another, all behavior of all species is very similar in all important aspects, and therefore we might as well use animals we can give shocks to, we do not have to pay, and whose lives we can completely control.

What is forgotten, among other things, is that each species is very different and that one generalizes at one's peril. Chickens are likely to starve to death if one inhibits their pecking for food past the developmental period when chickens naturally learn to peck. If, however, you keep swallows from flying long past the developmental period when swallows naturally learn to fly, they fly excellently at the first opportunity. This has been known for ninety years. Rats reared in darkness show no signs of impaired visual acuity when brought into light, whereas apes raised this way were functionally blind and only slowly regain visual ability. Fish are similar to apes in this regard; when raised in darkness they cannot respond to food on the basis of visual cues when moved to a lighted environment. Humans blind from birth, who later recover visual ability, respond like the apes; it takes them a considerable time to learn to use visual cues.

Which is a better model for humans in terms of the importance of developmental periods, chickens or swallows? By and large psychologists have chosen chickens because this fits in with what they wanted to believe on the basis of other theories they happened to be espousing at the time. There seems to have been no other particular reason or evidence for this choice.

So strong is the influence of an unverbalized assumption—in this case, that all behavior is basically composed of the same units and therefore is basically the same and that we can study the behavior of any organism, including humans, by studying a simpler organism—that even clear and hard evidence to the contrary does not change our thinking or our behavior.

This is demonstrated in a classic paper, "The Misbehavior of Organisms" by Kellar and Marian Breland. The Brelands are two animal psychologists who had, in 1961, published in *American Psychologist* a wholly affirmative and optimistic paper saying in essence that the principles derived from the laboratory could be applied to the extensive control of behavior under nonlaboratory conditions. They worked with a wide variety of species, including such unusual subjects as reindeer, cockatoos, raccoons, pigs, porpoises, and whales. What they found was that when they applied the principles of operant conditioning to these exotic species (but far less exotic than humans), they ran into a persistent pattern of failure.

This is critical to the validity of the whole concept of studying animals in order to understand man. The Brelands used the most basic and established techniques and concepts from the laboratory. These techniques should have worked on the subjects if there was any validity for the study of animals in the laboratory. They didn't. The implications are clear. They were ignored.

Typical of the Brelands' work was the following procedure, which works perfectly with white rats and pigeons. The animal is trained to press a bar. It receives (from a slot below the bar) a token adapted to the species: a "penny" of a size the animal species being studied can carry easily. The animal is further trained to take the token across the cage and deposit it in another slot. The animal then receives a reward of food: an apple for a pig, some grains of corn for a chicken, and so forth. Rats and pigeons continue this behavior once they have learned it for as long as they are hungry. When they get hungry again, they start the behavior again. There is no problem here and if you are a good Behaviorist psychologist, you understand how human beings function in the same way and learn, by means of identical conditioning and reward sequences, to paint the Mona Lisa, design a space suit, and march against apartheid.

The problem the Brelands ran into, however, was that their other species could learn how to press the bar, take the token across the cage, drop it in the slot, wait for the food, and then eat it, but after a few times in which they displayed their ability to do this sequence flawlessly, they stopped doing it and did something else. The pigs would still be very hungry, but after a few apples, they would take the large wooden pennies they were given and bring them to a corner of the cage (or enclosure they were worked in), drop them, and root around them. Why did they do this? Clearly, because they were pigs, not white rats. The chickens would learn the sequence, do it a few times, and then, still hungry, take their small wooden pennies, bring them to the center of the cage, drop them, and scratch around them. Why? They were chickens. That's why. Whales and porpoises would take their tokens—beach balls and inner tubes—across the pool a few times and then, still hungry, would toss them in the air and/or swallow them. And so forth up and down the range of the phylogenetic scale the Brelands explored. One might assume that human beings would learn the sequence easily and then, after a few times, would begin to pile the tokens against the wall in an attempt to climb out of the cage, try to use them as fuel to burn the walls of the cage down, play Frisbee with them, or something else at least as interesting as the use the pigs, chickens, and whales made of the tokens *they* received.

This major paper was written in a readable and humorous style. It came from an unimpeachable source. It was published in a place psychologists could not help seeing it. But it was ignored because it ran counter to the unverbalized assumption that the way to study a science was to make a model of your subject and then analyze the model. This idea works for molar physics and mechanics. It does not work for human beings.

The philosopher Ernst Cassirer (1946) has pointed out that the interpretation of myths has proved to be a magic mirror in which each school of interpreters sees only its own face or a reflection of what it wants and expects to see. Thus some schools see linguistic confusions, some the movements of the sun and moon, some unconscious statements of human sexual wishes and fears, some cosmic truths, and others a wide variety of other possibilities. Similarly, a metaphor for man is also a magic mirror reflecting only the wishes and expectations of believing that it reflects the subject of his study rather than a distorted caricature. The seven blind men and the elephant are a rather good metaphor for the psychologists who make metaphors for humankind.

A basic aspect of the problem for the human sciences is that, in this field, the model chosen reflects the temper of the times and the orientation of the particular scientist and has little to do with the subject itself. A "scientific" explanation of the behavior or a person tells us very little about the person but a great deal about the viewpoint, culture, and thinking of the explainer.

Once a metaphor for human beings, such as the rat or the computer, is set up and used, we are in an especially tricky and dangerous situation. "For once such parallels are set up, there is no way of curbing the reader's labyrinthine associations, no clear-cut check by which to separate actual from imaginary likenesses in interpretation (Madden 1962, p. 66).

One reason for the belief that humans and animals *must* be basically, qualitatively the same lies in the history of our culture. In the attempt to dethrone the religious view of reality of the Middle Ages and replace it with the "scientific" view of the Renaissance, it was deemed necessary to get rid of the concept of the soul. If animals and humans were qualitatively the same, then either gnats and flies had souls or humans did not. The logical conclusion was obvious once the premise was accepted.

And in the present age, when the average scientist seems as terrified of finding that he has a soul as a medieval monk would have been of finding out that he did not, it is a basic of the religion of science that there is only a quantitative difference between human and animal. Otherwise, humans, if *qualitatively* different from animals, might have souls (Swabey 1954, p. 25).

If we look deeply, many of the assumptions of modern science, assumptions that we accept without much verbalization or thought, turn out to be remnants of an old and long-past battle to get rid of a view of reality that has long since passed out of our world.

REFERENCES

Allport, G. (1940). The psychologist's frame of reference. *Psychological Bulletin* 37:14.

Arendt, H. (1958). *The Human Condition.* Chicago: University of Chicago Press.

Auden, W. H. (1947). *The Age of Anxiety.* New York: Simon & Schuster.

Beach, F. A. (1965). The snark was a boojum. In *Readings in Animal Behavior*, ed. T. E. McGill. New York: Holt, Rinehart & Winston.

Becker, E. (1969). *Angel in Armor.* New York: Free Press.

Berlin, I. (1981). Notes on alleged relationism in 18th century thought. In *Substance and Form in History*, ed. L. Pompa and W. H. Dray. Edinburgh: Edinburgh University Press.

Blanshard, B. (1939). *The Nature of Thought.* London: Allen & Unwin.

Boring, E. G. (1929). *The History of Experimental Psychology.* New York: Henry Holt.

Breland, K., and Breland, M. (1961). The misbehavior of organisms. *American Psychologist* 17:121–143.

Bronowski, J. (1978). *The Origins of Knowledge and Imagination*. New Haven, CT: Yale University Press.

Bugental, J. (1965). *The Search for Authenticity*. San Francisco: Jossey-Bass.

Burrow, T. (1932). Reply to Freud. In *Group Analysis* 13.

Cassirer, E. (1946). *The Myth of the State*. New Haven, CT: Yale University Press.

Cattell, J. M. (1895). Psychology as an experimental science. In *American Psychology in Historical Perspective*, ed. E. Hilgard. Washington, DC: American Psychological Association, 1978.

Chapanis, A. (1966). Men, machines, and models. In *Theories in Contemporary Psychology*, ed. R. H. Mark. New York: Macmillan.

Collingwood, R. (1940). *Human Nature and History*. New York: Basic Books.

De Gre, G. (1985). *The Social Compulsions of Ideas*. Oxford: Transaction Books.

Derogatis, L. R., Abeloff, M. R., and Melisantros, N. (1979). Coping mechanisms and survival time in metastatic breast cancer. *Journal of the American Medical Association* 242:1504–1508.

de Vries, M. (1994). Becoming Alive. Unpublished manuscript, Helen Dowling Institute, Rotterdam.

Dewey, J. (1910). *How We Think*. Boston: Heath.

Diagnostic and Statistical Manual of Mental Disorders (1994). 4th ed. Washington, DC: American Psychiatric Association.

Flam, N. (1994). The Jewish way of healing. *Reform Judaism* 22(4):36.

Frankl, V. (1959). *Man's Search for Meaning*. New York: Pocket Books.

Freud, S. (1932). Letter to S. H. Foulkes. *Group Analysis* 13:6–7.

—— (1937). Analysis terminable and interminable. *Standard Edition* 23.

Geertz, C. (1983). *Local Knowledge*. New York: Basic Books.

Heilbroner, R. L. (1959). *The Future as History*. New York: Harper.

Heinlein, R. (1985). *The Cat Who Walks through Walls*. New York: Putnam.

Hook, S., ed. (1966). *Dimensions of Mind*. New York: Collier, Macmillan.

Huxley, A. (1963). *The Door of Perception*. New York: Harper Colophon.

James, W. (1908). *Hibbert Lectures*. Manchester College, Oxford, May 4–26.

Kazantzakis, N. (1957). *Report to Greco*. Boston: Little, Brown.

Korzybski, A. (1951). Lecture to seminar, Lakeville, CT.

Kutscher, C. L. (1971). *Readings in Comparative Studies in Animal Behavior*. Waltham, MA: Xerox College Publishing.

Lehner, D. N. (1979). *Handbook of Ethological Methods*. New York: Garland STPM Press.

LeShan, L. (1990). *The Dilemma of Psychology: A Psychologist Looks at His Troubled Profession*. New York: Dutton.

Lindner, R. (1953). *Prescription for Rebellion*. London: Gollancz.

Madden, E. H. (1962). *Philosophical Problems of Psychology*. New York: Odyssey.

Malefist, A. D. W. (1974). *Images of Man*. New York: Knopf.

May, R. (1953). Historical and philosophical presuppositions in understanding therapy. In *Psychotherapy, Theory and Research*, ed. O. H. Mowrer. New York: Ronald.

McGraw, H. W., ed. (1934). *Prose and Poetry of America*. Chicago: Singer.

Merton, T. (1957). *No Man Is an Island*. New York: Dell.

—— (1961). *Spiritual Direction and Meditation*. Collegeville, MN: Liturgical Press.

Murphy, G. (1958). *Human Potentialities*. New York: Basic Books.

Perry, R. (1935). *The Thought and Character of William James*. Boston: Little, Brown.

Rank, O. (1948). *Will Therapy and Truth and Reality*. New York: Knopf. (Originally published 1929.)

Rogers, C. (1953). Some directions and end points in therapy. In *Psychotherapy, Theory and Research*, ed. O. H. Mowrer. New York: Ronald.

Rose, A. M. (1956). Conscious reactions associated with neuropsychiatric breakdown in combat. *Psychiatry* 19: 87–94.

Russell, B. (1929). *Our Knowledge of the External World.* New York: Norton.

Santayana, G. (1891). Review of William James's *Principles of Psychology. Atlantic* 66:555–556.

Sarason, S. (1981). *Psychology Misdirected.* New York: Free Press.

Schwartz, T. (1995). *What Really Matters: The Search for Wisdom in America.* New York: Bantam.

Searle, J. (1984). Minds, brains, and science. *Advances* 2(6):4.

Shedler, J., Mayman, M., and Manis, M. (1993). The illusion of mental health. *American Psychologist* 48(11):1117–1131.

Spiegel, H. (1974). The grade-5 syndrome: the highly hypnotizable person. *International Journal of Clinical Hypnosis* 22:303–319.

Spiegel, H., and Greenleaf, M. (1992). Personality style and hypnotizability: the fix-flex continuum. *Psychiatric Medicine* 10:13–23.

Spiegel, H., and Shainess, G. (1963). Operational Spectrum of psychotherapeutic process. *Archives of General Psychiatry* 9:477–488.

Spiegel, H., and Spiegel, D. (1978). *Trance and Treatment.* New York: Basic Books.

Stevenson, A. (1965). Talk at the United Nations Economic and Social Council, Geneva, July 9.

Swabey, M. C. (1954). *The Judgement of History.* New York: Philosophical Library.

Szasz, T. (1958). The myth of mental illness. *American Psychologist* 13:115.

Turner, G. H. (1960). Psychology—becoming and unbecoming. *Canadian Journal of Psychology* 14:155.

Watson, G. (1958). Moral issues in psychotherapy. *American Psychologist* 13:575.

West, M. (1984). *The World Is Made of Glass*. New York: Avon.

White, T. H. (1977). *The Book of Merlyn*. Austin: University of Texas Press.

Willis, R. (1994). *Transcendence in Relationship, Existentialism and Psychotherapy*. Norwood, NJ: Ablex.

Yeats, W. B. (1899). He wishes for the cloths of heaven. In *The Variorum Edition of the Poems of W. B. Yeats*, ed. P. Alt and R. K. Alspach. New York: Macmillan, 1940, p. 176.

INDEX